DYSLEXIA
AND OTHER
LEARNING DIFFICULTIES

the**facts**

Second Edition

Mark Selikowitz
Consultant Developmental Paediatrician
Sydney, Australia

Oxford   New York   Tokyo
OXFORD UNIVERSITY PRESS
1998

Oxford University Press, Great Clarendon Street, Oxford, OX2 6DP

Oxford   New York
Athens   Auckland   Bangkok   Bogota   Bombay   Buenos Aires
Calcutta   Cape Town   Dar es Salaam   Delhi   Florence
Hong Kong   Istanbul   Karachi   Kuala Lumpur   Madras
Madrid   Melbourne   Mexico City   Nairobi   Paris
Singapore   Taipei   Tokyo   Toronto   Warsaw

and associated companies in
Berlin   Ibadan

Oxford is a trade mark of Oxford University Press

Published in the United States
by Oxford University Press Inc., New York

First edition published 1993
Reprinted 1993, 1994, 1995, 1996
Second edition published 1998

© Mark Selikowitz, 1998

A catalogue record for this book is available from the British Library

Library of Congress Cataloging in Publication Data
(Data applied for)

ISBN 0 19 262661 2

Typeset by EXPO Holdings, Malaysia

Printed in Great Britain by Biddles Ltd., Guildford, Surrey

Preface

In the preface to the first edition of this book, I stated that my intention was to produce an easy-to-read guide that covered specific learning difficulties in a balanced and comprehensive manner. For this second edition I have tried to ensure that this intention has again been followed.

To ensure that the book would retain its accessibility to parents, changes have only been made where information has become out of date, or where important new developments have occurred. An example of such a development has been the considerable shift in thinking about the treatment of milder forms of coexisting attention difficulties in children with reading difficulties.

There is even more reason to be optimistic about the future for people with specific learning difficulties than when the first edition was written. This is a result of the many new developments in diagnostic methods, multimodal treatment programmes, and vocational training opportunities for people with specific learning difficulties. There is no doubt that the child or adult with specific learning difficulty can now benefit from more appropriate assistance than at any time in the past.

Sydney   M.S.
January 1998

Preface to the first edition

This book has been written for parents. I hope that it will also prove of interest to professionals, and indeed anyone interested in why some intelligent children struggle to learn.

My intention has been to write an easy-to-read guide that covers specific learning difficulties in a balanced and comprehensive manner. I have concentrated on information that is of practical relevance to parents in understanding their children's difficulties and in helping them to overcome these. The emphasis is on accurate diagnosis and simple, conventional ways of helping children gain skills and improve self-esteem.

The four chapters in Part I of the book cover specific learning difficulties in a general way: defining terms, describing diagnostic methods, explaining theories of causation, and giving a general guide to the way parents can help their child. These chapters should be read by all parents.

Each of the eight chapters in Part II of the book is devoted to a specific area of learning, and parents can select those chapters that are relevant to their child's particular difficulties.

Part III contains a chapter discussing controversial treatments and a chapter dealing with persisting specific learning difficulties in adulthood. These chapters should be of interest to all parents.

To avoid using the cumbersome 'he or she' when referring to the child with a specific learning difficulty, I have used only 'he'. My justification for this compromise is that in this condition males outnumber females by approximately three to one. All statements apply equally to both sexes unless otherwise specified.

Preface to the first edition

I am grateful to Mr Marcus Cremonese, Graphic Designer at the Medical Illustration Unit, University of New South Wales Teaching Hospitals, who prepared all the drawings and charts.

The sample of text in Figure 3 is reproduced from *Pitman i.t.a. Early-to-Read Program*, by Mazurkiewicz and Tanzer (1967). It is reproduced with the permission of the publisher, Longman-Cheshire.

Among colleagues whose comments have helped me, I would particularly like to thank Mrs J. Sunman, who read the first version of the typescript and made several valuable suggestions. Mrs N. Fletcher kindly proof-read the final typescript.

I am grateful to the staff at Oxford University Press for their support.

Lastly, I thank my wife, Jill, for her encouragement and advice, and my children, Daniel and Anne, for their patience while this book was being written.

Sydney   M.S.
June 1992

the**facts**

CONTENTS

Contents

Part 1

Introduction

1
What are specific learning difficulties?

Angela is 10 years old. Her parents describe her as a 'bright' girl. Nevertheless, Angela's teacher has told her parents that her reading ability is well below that of the rest of the class. Testing by a psychologist found Angela's reading to be at a seven-year-old level and her intelligence to be normal. Her vision has been tested and is also normal. She is well motivated and well adjusted emotionally. Neither the psychologist, nor her doctor, could find any reason why she should have difficulty reading. Her parents are puzzled and concerned.

Michael is eight years old. He is a healthy, energetic boy whom his parents describe as 'an active, outdoor boy—always on the go'. They have learned to give him scope for burning off his excess energy at home. But problems have now arisen at school. His writing is illegible, and the teacher complains that he never sits still. He is making little progress in school work, and continually getting into trouble for being disruptive in class. A psychologist has found that he is unable to form legible letters, despite making great efforts to do so. She tested his intelligence and found it to be in the normal range. A doctor has examined him and found no cause for his difficulties.

This is a book about children like Angela and Michael: intelligent children who have a significant and un-explained difficulty in learning.

Every child with such difficulties is unique, but they have enough in common with one another for their condition to be summarized by one collective term. I shall use the term 'specific learning difficulties' as an umbrella term for this whole group of disorders.

Defining specific learning difficulties

A specific learning difficulty can be defined as:

> an unexpected and *unexplained* condition, occurring in a child of *average* or *above average intelligence*, characterized by a *significant delay* in one or more *areas of learning*.

In order to understand this definition fully, a number of important questions must be answered. Which areas of learning are involved? What is a 'significant delay'? Which other causes of difficulty must be excluded? Let us look at these questions one by one.

Which areas of learning are involved?

The areas of learning involved in specific learning difficulties can be divided into two groups.

The first group consists of the basic academic skills: reading, writing, spelling, arithmetic, and language (both comprehension and expression). These are relatively easy skills to measure, and are of central importance to success at school.

The second group contains areas of learning that are also vitally important, but are far less well understood. These involve the learning of skills such as persistence, organization, impulse control, social competence, and the coordination of movements.

I shall use the term specific learning difficulty to cover significant delay in any of these areas. Children may have only one area involved, or a number of areas. I am, therefore, using the term 'learning' in a broad sense, to include all areas of learning, not only academic areas.

There are good reasons for grouping all these difficulties together. It has been well established that difficulties in these different areas of learning are closely related. They often coexist in the same child, they are all more common in boys, they all share the same theories of causation, and they all share the same general principles of management. In a book for parents, this broad approach is particularly useful, because parents are interested in all their child's difficulties in learning, both at school and at home.

What is a 'significant delay'?

If the term specific learning difficulty is to have any meaning, it should be used only for children who have marked difficulties in learning, that are beyond the average range. We should not use the term for children whose difficulties are merely part of the normal variation. These should be regarded as variations in talent, rather than significant difficulties. But how do we decide what is the average range? This is not a problem unique to specific learning difficulties, but one that arises whenever we try to define any disorder.

There are two sets of criteria that are used to make the distinction between the average range and below this range. The set of criteria used in the diagnosis of a specific learning difficulty depends on the particular area of learning involved.

Statistical criteria

In areas of learning that lend themselves to precise measurement of achievement, such as reading, spelling, and arithmetic, we can measure the child's ability using a standardized test. This is a test that has been performed in exactly the same way on many children to develop standards (norms) for different ages. In this manner, a particular child can be tested and given a score that compares his performance with that of his peers.

A range of scores is usually designated as the average range for any such test. A score below this range would be regarded as indicative of a significant delay.

There are certain conventions governing how this average range is selected for a standardized test.[1] The nature of these tests will be described in the relevant chapters of Part 2.

Clinical criteria

Many skills do not lend themselves to accurate quantification. In such situations it is necessary to rely on careful evaluation of the child's ability and behaviour by one or more professionals with the experience and training necessary to assess the significance of a child's difficulties. When clinical criteria are used, it is best if assessment is based on the child's abilities and behaviour in a number of different situations. This will be discussed further in the next chapter.

Are these criteria reliable?

The existence of specific learning difficulties is sometimes questioned because of the arbitrary nature of these criteria. It is true that both the above methods do require an arbitrary decision about what constitutes a significant difficulty in learning. However, this arbitrariness is no greater for specific learning difficulties than for most other conditions in children and adults. For example, the diagnosis of conditions such as anaemia, high blood pressure, and obesity are all based on statistical criteria that have an arbitrary cut-off point to distinguish normal values from abnormal values. The diagnosis of conditions such as

---

[1] It is usual to define below average as '*more than two standard deviations below the mean*'. This is roughly equivalent to saying that the child's abilities must be below that of approximately 97.5 per cent of children of his age.

Another definition of 'significant delay' is that the child's achievement in the affected area of learning is *two or more years behind his chronological age*. This is not a good definition, because two years is a relatively greater delay in a younger child than in an older child.

epilepsy, migraine, and asthma are based on clinical criteria that are no less subjective, or difficult to define, than
those used for the diagnosis of specific learning difficulties.
(A group of experts, meeting in 1972 in order to define
asthma, came to the conclusion that they were unable to
do so; yet all agreed that they could recognize it when
they saw it.) In the final analysis, the validity of any diagnosis rests on the expertise of the person, or persons, making the diagnosis.

Which other causes of difficulty must be excluded?

Specific learning difficulties should, strictly speaking, be
called *idiopathic* specific learning difficulties, which means
that their cause is unknown. In practice the word 'idiopathic' is omitted, but its meaning is inferred.

The diagnosis of a specific learning difficulty is, therefore, partly a diagnosis of exclusion. The term should not
be used until all other recognized causes of poor academic
achievement have been excluded. These include sensory
impairments (vision and hearing defects), motor handi-
caps (such as cerebral palsy and muscular dystrophy),
environmental disadvantage (poor teaching, prolonged or
frequent absence from school, adverse cultural factors),
and emotional disturbances. The exclusion of these
conditions calls for considerable expertise, and should
involve professionals from more than one discipline, as
will be explained in the next chapter.

How early can specific learning difficulties be diagnosed?

Specific learning difficulties are usually diagnosed when a
child is at school; they often do not become evident until
more demanding academic work is required, from the age
of eight years onwards.

There have been claims that children who will have
specific learning difficulties can be identified in the

pre-school years: one psychologist has even developed a test that he claims detects specific learning difficulties in newborn babies. These claims must be regarded with caution.

Children of pre-school age vary tremendously in their abilities, and so tests of development at this age are poor predictors of later ability. Any attempt to identify pre-school-aged children who are destined to have specific learning difficulties will engender unnecessary anxiety in parents, while missing many of the children who will have specific learning difficulties. It is also important to realize that treatment during the pre-school years (known as early intervention) has not been proven to prevent or ameliorate the later development of specific learning difficulties.

Children of pre-school age who are delayed in their development should be seen by a paediatrician and may benefit from early intervention, but they should not be considered to have a specific learning difficulty at this early age. Programmes to detect children with 'early' specific learning difficulties, prior to school age, are unjustified in the light of our present knowledge.

In this book, therefore, I shall confine my attention to children of school age.

Historical background

Difficulty with reading was the first form of specific learning difficulty to be described. In 1878, a German physician, Dr Kussmaul, described a man who was unable to learn to read. The man was of normal intelligence and had received an adequate education. Dr Kussmaul called this problem *reading blindness*. Nine years later, Dr Berlin, another German doctor, coined the term *dyslexia* (from the Greek for 'difficulty with words') for this condition.

The first British report of a specific learning difficulty was also of adults with reading difficulty. A Scottish eye surgeon, Dr James Hinshelwood, published the report in 1895, and called the condition *word blindness*. His paper prompted the first description of specific reading difficulty in a child, one year later, when Dr Pringle Morgan described a 14-year-old boy, Percy, with reading difficulty. The boy's teacher wrote that '[he] would be the smartest lad in the school if instruction were entirely oral'.

During the first quarter of the twentieth century, interest continued to focus on specific reading difficulty. In 1925, an American neurologist, Dr Samuel T. Orton, proposed the first theory of how specific reading difficulty arose. He placed great emphasis on the development of dominance of one side of the brain. This theory will be discussed further in Chapter 3. Together with his assistant, Anna Gillingham, he developed a number of teaching strategies, some of which are still in use.

Other forms of specific learning difficulty were also described during this period, but these were not widely recognized until 1939, when Dr Alfred Strauss and Dr Heinz Werner published their description of children with a wide range of learning difficulties. They emphasized the variety of these problems and the importance of looking at each child individually to assess their particular educational needs. It was their work that gave the impetus to the establishment of clinical and educational services for children with specific learning difficulties, first in North America, and then in other parts of the world.

A landmark was reached in 1977, when Public Law 94-142 was passed in the USA, ensuring the rights of American children with specific learning difficulties to appropriate evaluation and management of their problem. In 1981, the United Kingdom passed an Education Act that stated that children with learning difficulties of all kinds were entitled to appropriate evaluation and help according to their special needs.

Specific learning difficulties now receive much more attention than at any other time in the past. There are a number of reasons for this:

- At no other time in history has the ability to gain academic skills and qualifications been such an important factor in a highly competitive employment market.

- All children in developed countries now attend school, and parents take an interest in their progress.

- The need for proficiency in academic skills has extended beyond urban areas, as work in rural areas has also become more technical and competitive.

- With the reduction in the number of serious illnesses that affect children (such as polio and TB), more attention can now be directed towards the non-life-threatening problems such as specific learning difficulties.

- There has been a realization that some of the emotional problems of adolescence and adulthood relate to school difficulties and that if not properly managed during childhood, such difficulties may play an important part in impairing self-esteem and the ability to cope in later life.

- With the realization that many developmental and behavioural problems have underlying biological causes, the search for such causes in conditions such as specific learning difficulties has intensified. Children with these difficulties are thus less likely to be dismissed as lazy, as was the case in the past.

Terms used for types of specific learning difficulty

It will be apparent that the term specific learning difficulties covers a group of disorders. Children may have problems in one area of learning, or in a number of different areas. Some disorders have a tendency to cluster together in children, so that spelling difficulties often accompany reading difficulties, and arithmetic difficulties often accompany language difficulties—but any combination can occur.

One of the major causes of confusion to parents is the wide number of terms used for the different forms of specific learning difficulty. To make matters worse, the same term may be used by different people to mean different things. This sometimes reflects the fact that specific learning difficulties are of interest to a wide range of professionals, such as doctors, educators, and psychologists, and that each discipline has its own perspective and its own terminology.

The term *dyslexia*, as mentioned above, was first coined in 1887 to describe isolated reading difficulty. Unfortunately, the word has been widely used in an inconsistent way. Some still use it for specific reading difficulty alone, others for combined reading and writing difficulties, while others use it for all types of specific learning difficulty.

There are similar Greek terms for other forms of specific learning difficulty. Specific spelling difficulty is called *dysorthographia*; specific writing difficulty is called *dysgraphia*; and specific arithmetic difficulty is referred to as *dyscalculia*. I shall avoid these terms and use the English equivalents.

Children with attention problems are sometimes described as having *attention deficit disorder*, with or without *hyperactivity*. I shall discuss both these terms in Chapter 10.

There are also terms such as *minimal brain damage* and *strephosymbolia* that are used for specific learning difficulties. These are based on certain theories of causation and will be explained in Chapter 3. 'Specific learning difficulty' has the advantage that it does not suggest a cause, but simply describes the nature of the child's problem.

How common are specific learning difficulties?

The number of children who have a specific learning difficulty is unknown. To determine this it would be necessary to carry out a thorough survey in which all the children in a population were carefully assessed to detect those who had any form of specific learning difficulty. This has not been done. However, there have been surveys to detect difficulties in individual areas of learning. This allows one to piece together some estimate of the frequency of the condition as a whole.

In this way it can be estimated that about 10 per cent of children have some form of specific learning difficulty. The most commonly involved areas of learning are reading, language, attention, and motor coordination. These occur in approximately equal proportions.

There is some evidence that certain specific learning difficulties are less common in some countries. This may be owing to differences in the way data are collected, or it may reflect genetic differences. It may also be a result of differences in the education system. Certain characteristics of the language may play a part in some countries. For example, the low stated prevalence of specific reading difficulty in Japan may be related to the nature of the Japanese writing system, which does not require the same degree of phonological skills as, for example, English.

Fortunately, mild forms of specific learning difficulty are far more common than severe forms. For example, only about two per cent of children with specific reading difficulty have a severe form of this condition.

Boys are approximately three times more likely to be affected by any form of specific learning difficulty. This is thought to be a consequence of certain genes on the X chromosome (see Chapter 3).

It is often stated that specific learning difficulty is a 'middle-class' disorder, but this is not the case. Surveys have generally found a constant frequency of affected children across the full range of socio-economic categories. The impression that middle-class children are more frequently affected may have arisen because parents from disadvantaged families are less likely to seek help for their child's poor school attainments. It is also possible that middle-class parents, with their greater emphasis on academic achievement, are more likely to seek an excuse for their child's poor attainments. They may, therefore, use the term 'dyslexia' too readily. Used in this way, the term will cease to have any meaning. This is why proper diagnosis is essential.

The benefits of recognizing specific learning difficulties

The label 'specific learning difficulty', if correctly used, has a number of benefits. It gives parents the satisfaction of knowing that their child's problem is a recognized entity: that it is not their fault, nor the fault of their child. This means that they do not have to keep searching for a reason for their child's difficulties. This is important because children with a specific learning difficulty are so capable in some ways, and yet have such unexpected difficulties in others, that it is easy to think that the child is simply being lazy or has been poorly taught. Having a name for the problem also enables parents to benefit from the knowledge gained by others with experience of the condition. It enables groups to be set up so that parents can share information and support one another. These groups can also lobby for legislation that ensures that these children's special needs are catered for. Research into specific learning difficulties can be undertaken, thereby increasing our understanding of the condition and enabling us to find effective ways of helping these children.

However, this label can also have disadvantages if incorrectly used. The diagnosis of a specific learning difficulty should be made with care. It is not a term to be used for every child who fails at school or behaves badly. Even when the diagnosis has been properly made, care should still be taken. It should be borne in mind that this is not a single disorder, but a group of related disorders. Each child with a specific learning difficulty is unique and the diagnostic process should include an assessment of his individual abilities and needs. This will be described in the next chapter.

2

How a specific learning difficulty is diagnosed

In many cases it is the teacher who first suspects that a child may have a specific learning difficulty. Teachers are able to compare a child's work and behaviour to that of his peers, and so can often spot a child who is experiencing difficulties before this is noticed by his parents.

Sometimes, however, parents are the first to realize that their child may have a problem. There is no completely reliable way of detecting that your child has a specific learning difficulty, but here are some pointers that may alert you to the need for further evaluation of your child's difficulties.

Pointers to a specific learning difficulty

It is quite normal for a child to struggle with skills such as reading, writing, spelling, and arithmetic in the first year or two of school, but after this period, he should attain a basic level of competence. If your child continues to struggle beyond this period, he may have a specific learning difficulty. This should be suspected if he seems to be out of his depth and is not showing signs of becoming competent in basic academic skills. It may also be apparent to you that he seems brighter than these difficulties in his academic work would suggest.

His reading may be slow and hesitant, with elementary errors. When reading, he may make up the story based on the illustrations to cover his difficulties, or he may guess wildly at words. He may be unable to spell the words in his spelling list, despite trying reasonably hard. His writing may remain very immature or illegible despite his best efforts. Another warning sign is a child who can write neatly, but only if he writes at an extremely slow speed.

If his arithmetic skills are affected, he will seem to be lost when asked to do the calculations expected of a child in his class. He may have great difficulties understanding the meaning of arithmetical operations such as addition, subtraction, and multiplication.

Another clue that a child may have a specific learning difficulty is speech delay. The child may struggle to express himself, or his speech may be immature and indistinct. Sometimes it is the child's difficulty in understanding language that is noticed first. He may become confused if given a complex instruction, and may not understand stories that are appropriate for his age.

Parents may notice that their child has difficulties in other areas of his development. Clumsiness, poor organization, poor concentration, and lack of self-control are all signs that a specific learning difficulty may be present. He may be restless and impulsive, and unable to concentrate on one task for an appropriate period of time. He may have great difficulty getting things in the right order, or learning to differentiate right from left. Skills such as learning to do his shoe laces and tell the time may be beyond him at an age when other children are mastering these with ease.

Sometimes a specific learning difficulty presents first as a behaviour problem, or as a difficulty with peer relationships. This is a trap for the unwary as the problem may be put down to naughtiness, and the underlying learning difficulty not suspected. The child may refuse to do school work or he may truant. He may become withdrawn, or aggressive and defiant. He may be rejected by other children and become socially isolated. These behaviours may indicate low self-esteem as a result of difficulties with school work, or they may indicate a social immaturity that is itself a form of specific learning difficulty (this will be described in Chapter 12). Difficulty with concentration that results in restlessness and impulsivity may also be misinterpreted as naughtiness.

What to do if you suspect that your child has a specific learning difficulty

If you suspect that your child has a specific learning difficulty, arrange to speak to his teacher. Make a time when you can discuss your concerns with him or her in private. At the meeting, find out how your child behaves at school and how he compares with his peers, both in his academic work and in other areas of competence. Ask the teacher whether an evaluation of your child's problem is needed.

Although parents and teachers are the ones who first suspect that a child may have a specific learning difficulty, making the definitive diagnosis is not something that you, or the teacher, should try to do. If it is clear that your child is experiencing significant difficulties, then a comprehensive assessment, as outlined below, should be arranged.

What is a comprehensive assessment?

A comprehensive assessment is a process whereby the exact nature of a child's learning difficulties is established. In such an assessment the child's precise strengths and weaknesses are ascertained, and it is determined whether a cause for his difficulties can be found. In addition, appropriate methods of treatment are planned.

A comprehensive assessment requires the expertise of both an educational psychologist and a paediatrician, working in close cooperation. The roles of these professionals complement one another in establishing the nature and cause of the child's difficulties. It is important that both the psychologist and the paediatrician have experience in the diagnosis and management of learning difficulties.

In many children with specific learning difficulties, a speech therapist, physiotherapist, or occupational therapist also plays an important part in the assessment. In children with language difficulties, an assessment by a speech therapist is essential. In children with handwriting difficulties, an occupational therapist's assessment is usually needed. Children who are clumsy often need to be assessed by both an occupational therapist and a physiotherapist. If a child needs to see any of these therapists, this can be arranged by the psychologist or paediatrician who does the initial assessment.

The important roles of these therapists will be defined and discussed in later chapters that deal with specific areas of learning. In this chapter, assessment by the psychologist and doctor are described.

How to arrange an assessment

Assessments are a legal right for children with 'special educational needs' in the UK, and children with 'specific learning disabilities' in the USA. Even when this is not the case, it is usually easy to arrange an assessment in countries such as Australia, Canada, New Zealand, the Republic of Ireland, and South Africa. There are three ways in which an assessment can be arranged.

Education department

In the UK, the 1981 Education Act allows parents to request a free assessment for their child if he has 'special educational needs' (that is, significantly greater difficulty in learning than the majority of children of his age).

In the USA, a free evaluation prior to the drawing up of an educational plan is one of the key provisions of Public Law 94-142. This law defines 'specific learning disability' in much the same way that specific learning difficulties have been defined in this book.

In the UK and USA, parental involvement in the assessment is ensured by legislation. In these countries, the Education Department has to seek medical advice about the child, usually from the child's own doctor. In other counties, Education Departments usually have psychologists who will assess children with learning difficulties.[1]

If you want your child to be assessed by an educational psychologist from the Education Department then ask your child's teacher how this can be arranged. It will also be necessary for you to ask your family doctor to arrange a separate referral to a paediatrician with an interest in learning difficulties. It is important that this paediatrician liaises with the educational psychologist who assesses your child.

Learning difficulties clinics

Learning difficulties clinics, or 'dyslexia clinics' as they are sometimes known, exist in children's hospitals in most parts of the world. They are staffed by paediatricians, psychologists, social workers, and sometimes nurses, therapists, and teachers. They provide a 'one-stop' assessment of your child's abilities by a number of professionals from different disciplines, working as a team. They usually have close links with education authorities, and their findings are invariably accepted without the need to duplicate tests. The multidisciplinary staff has extensive knowledge and experience of children with a wide range of learning difficulties.

Many parents prefer to have their child assessed at such a clinic, even where Education Department assessments are available. They prefer the convenience of seeing all the professionals at one time. This approach also allows more open communication for all concerned.

Perhaps the greatest advantage is that this type of assessment is not confined to educational issues alone. A

---

[1] In Australia, such psychologists may be called 'school counsellors'.

wide range of problems experienced by parents can be discussed. Members of the assessment team are able to provide information about other services such as social skills groups and parent support groups. They can also advise about behaviour management, and will be able to give you information about alternative school options (both government and private) if necessary.

You may be able to find out about such a clinic through your child's teacher or your family doctor. The organizations listed in the Appendix should also be able to direct you to such a clinic. Another way to find your local learning difficulties clinic is to phone the nearest children's hospital.

Developmental paediatricians and psychologists in private practice

There are educational psychologists in private practice who will test your child, for a fee, and report their findings to you. In this situation, it will be necessary for your family doctor to arrange for you to see a developmental paediatrician separately. The developmental paediatrician and educational psychologist will need to liaise with one another to ensure a coordinated approach.

Some psychologists and developmental paediatricians in private practice have formed private learning difficulties clinics analogous to those described above.

How a diagnostic assessment is carried out

The psychologist and paediatrician will carry out the assessment in four stages:

- collection of information about the child
- examination (testing) of the child
- explanation of the findings to the parents
- recommendation of an appropriate management plan.

Collection of information about the child

Prior to the assessment visit

'Assessment' is a word that often makes parents feel anxious. They are concerned that important decisions about their child's future may be based on his performance on a particular day. Any good assessment will, however, take into account the parents', therapists', and teachers' reports about a child's skills and behaviour demonstrated in the past, and in a wide range of situations.

You may, therefore, receive a request from the psychologist or paediatrician, prior to the assessment day, for permission to obtain reports from the teacher, and any other professionals who have seen your child in the past. If you do not receive such a request, it is a good idea to ask the professionals who have seen your child to provide you with reports so that you can show these to the psychologist and paediatrician when you take your child for assessment.

The psychologist and paediatrician will also want to ensure that your child has adequate vision and hearing. It is a good idea to have both of these things checked prior to the assessment. This should be done even if vision and hearing seem to be good in everyday situations, as minor difficulties are easily missed and may play a role in a child's difficulties. Your family doctor will be able to arrange a referral to an ophthalmologist (a doctor specializing in eye disorders) and an audiologist (a technician trained to test hearing). If this cannot be organized before the assessment, the paediatrician who carries out the assessment will arrange for such testing to be done after the assessment.

At the assessment

It is best if both parents attend the assessment. This enables both of them to give their views about the child, and to hear the results and recommendations first hand.

The psychologist and the paediatrician will collect information about your child. They will want to know your concerns about your child, his progress in the past, and your future plans for his education. They will ask you for your views on your child's problems. They will also be interested in information about any special help he has received. They will rely on you to provide a picture of the skills and behaviour that he demonstrates at home and when out. They will ask questions about his health. Information will also be collected on any relevant health or developmental problems in other members of the family. All of this information, together with reports from other professionals who have seen your child, form an essential part of the assessment.

Examination of the child—the psychologist's role

Approach to testing

After collecting information from you, the psychologist will want to spend time with your child, getting to know him in an unstructured setting. He or she will then want to administer some standardized tests. These are known as 'psychometric tests', and they measure the child's abilities and compare them to those of other children of the same age.

It is very important to watch your child being tested. This demystifies the process, and helps you to understand how the psychologist comes to his or her conclusions. It also enables you to inform the psychologist if your child's performance was not up to his usual standard.

In order to observe testing, it is best if you watch through a one-way screen so that your presence does not distract the child. Children can be shown the screen and told what it is before testing starts; they usually become used to it and ignore it once they become absorbed in testing. If a one-way screen is unavailable, you will need to discuss with the psychologist whether you should remain in the room. If you do, sit some way behind your child and be careful not to become involved in the testing; smile at your child in an encouraging way if he turns to look at you, but do not say anything. When the test is finished, the psychologist will give you time to comment on your child's performance, out of your child's hearing.

Tests of ability, particularly intelligence tests, have come in for criticism over the last few years; however, they still form an important part of establishing a child's abilities and needs. They must be performed by an experienced psychologist, and interpreted with care. The results of the test should be regarded as only part of the child's assessment and need to be interpreted in the light of reports of his abilities at other times and the results of any previous tests.

The tests that are generally used have been administered to many hundreds of children to obtain standards for different ages. Tasks are presented in a specific order, with the easier ones first. They then become progressively more advanced, to establish at what level they become too difficult for the child. Every child who does the test would be presented with tasks that are easy, as well as tasks that are too difficult for him. This is necessary in order to find out the exact level at which he is functioning.

During the course of the test, a picture of the child's developmental progress can be formed, both for specific areas of development and for development as a whole. Sometimes, a great deal of information can be gained from the way in which the child tackles tasks, even if he is unable to succeed. For example, the psychologist will observe his ability to persist with tasks, his ability to attend for long periods, and his ability to sit still.

One of the frustrating things for parents watching their child being tested, is that the way in which the tester asks questions, and presents puzzles and other materials, cannot be varied. As standards for children of different ages were developed by administering the tests in a particular way, the test must be carried out in the same way if these standards are to remain valid. Parents often feel that their child would have been able to succeed at a task, had the tester worded the questions differently or given some extra assistance. While the psychologist should be interested in these observations by the parent, only responses to the standard way of testing can be scored. Many of the skills needed in the classroom require the ability to perform tasks in very specific ways; testing may demonstrate that the child lacks the ability to adapt to such circumstances.

Sometimes, testing in a one-to-one situation does not give the psychologist enough information about the child's difficulties. He or she may then need to visit the school and observe the child in the classroom. Permission to visit must be sought from the school principal. It is usually best if the visit is arranged in such a way that the other children regard the psychologist as visiting the class as a whole, rather than having one child singled out.

Types of test used

Each psychologist will choose the test, or tests, that he or she considers the most useful for the particular child. There are now many tests available and a psychologist need only become familiar with a selected number of these. The tests used in children with known, or suspected, specific learning difficulties can be divided into three basic types:

- tests of intelligence
- tests of academic achievement
- tests of other special abilities.

Tests of intelligence

These tests contain many items that assess general intelligence. Some are ideally suited to children with learning difficulties because they do not involve reading or writing at all. They can, therefore, test intelligence irrespective of academic achievement. An intelligence test will not only establish the child's level of intelligence, but also give valuable information about some of his strengths and weaknesses.

The different tasks in the test are usually grouped into a number of 'sub-tests'; the score of each sub-test reflects a particular area of intelligence. The sub-tests for one of the commonest intelligence tests for school-aged children, the Wechsler Intelligence Scale for Children (WISC), are grouped together to give a 'verbal' score, which is a measure of the child's ability in language-related tasks, and a 'performance' score, which is related to visual and manual tasks. A comparison of these scores will show if a child is having particular difficulties in one of these areas.

Tests of academic achievement

These include tests of reading, spelling, and mathematics. In a child with learning difficulties, it will usually be necessary for the psychologist to perform one or more of these tests in addition to the intelligence test.

Academic achievement tests establish the level of a child's skills in a particular area of learning compared with his peers, and also give important information about the nature of a child's difficulties in the area tested. These tests will be described in the relevant chapters dealing with difficulties in specific skills (Chapters 5–8).

Tests of other special abilities

There are other tests carried out in children with learning difficulties. These include tests of language (which may be performed by a speech therapist). Language tests will be described in Chapter 9.

There are also tests of motor (movement) proficiency, which may be performed by a psychologist, a doctor, an occupational therapist, or a physiotherapist. These will be described in Chapter 11.

Psychologists also carry out a number of tests to evaluate specific areas of ability that play a role in learning.

These include visual perception, auditory discrimination, and sequential organization. These will be explained in later chapters. The interpretation of the results of these tests may give the child's teacher valuable ideas about ways of helping him.

Examination of the child—the paediatrician's role

After collecting information from the parents (referred to as taking a history), the paediatrician will examine the child (referred to as, performing a 'physical examination'). He or she may also arrange for some special tests to be performed, depending on the findings of the history and the physical examination.

In taking a history and examining the child, the paediatrician will call upon his or her knowledge of the many conditions that can cause learning impairment. In most cases, no cause will be found, but such a search is essential if certain rare, treatable causes of poor academic achievement are not to be missed. The causes of learning impairment that have to be excluded are listed in Table 1.

In some children, one of the conditions listed in Table 1 may be present but may not adequately explain the

Table 1 Causes of learning impairment that must be excluded before a diagnosis of specific learning disability can be made

Vision or hearing impairment
Intellectual disability
Physical disability (e.g. cerebral palsy)
Lack of familiarity with the language of instruction
Lack of family support
Poor teaching
Lack of motivation
Frequent absenteeism
Brain damage (e.g. following head trauma or meningitis)
Petit mal epilepsy
Medicines or drugs that impair learning

child's poor academic achievement. The condition may then be acting as an aggravating factor in a child whose primary problem is a specific learning difficulty. Poor motivation is a particular trap for the unwary, as many children with specific learning difficulties become poorly motivated or truant *as a result* of their difficulties. In such cases, their poor school attainments may be incorrectly attributed to poor motivation or school absences alone. It often requires careful judgement by the paediatrician and psychologist to determine whether a particular problem is the only cause of the child's difficulties, or is an aggravating factor in a child with an underlying specific learning difficulty.

The physical examination

The paediatrician will check the child's growth (height, weight, and head size). He or she will search for any unusual features in the child's body that suggest one of the rare genetic syndromes that are occasionally associated with specific learning difficulties.

He or she will examine the nervous system with particular care, looking for clear evidence of any abnormality ('hard neurological signs'). This is done by checking the child's coordination and balance, as well as his muscular strength, tone, and reflexes. The paediatrician also tests the functioning of the various nerves in the body.

The paediatrician may also look for other so-called 'soft neurological signs', which are more subtle evidence of difficulties in processing sensations and controlling movement. Although these signs are more common in children with specific learning difficulties, they may also be present in children without learning difficulties. They do not have the same implications as hard neurological signs and their significance remains controversial.

Special tests

There are a number of special tests that the paediatrician may arrange for a child with learning difficulties in certain circumstances. With the exception of tests of vision and hearing, none of these tests is mandatory; the doctor will only request them if something about the child's problems makes them necessary.

Vision and hearing tests

The testing of vision and hearing is essential in every child with learning difficulties. Even though the child may seem to see and hear well in everyday circumstances, careful testing may detect minor defects of vision or hearing that could play an important role in impairing his learning. Although some paediatricians have the equipment to test a child's vision and hearing, in most cases it will be necessary for the vision to be tested by an ophthalmologist, and the hearing to be tested by an audiologist.

The audiologist will test the hearing in a soundproof room. The child is fitted with headphones and tested with sounds of varying frequency and volume.

Referral to the ophthalmologist and audiologist can be arranged by the paediatrician, if this has not already been done by the family doctor.

Chromosome test

Very rarely, learning difficulties may be associated with a defect on the chromosomes. These are tiny, rod-shaped structures that carry the genes. They are present in every cell of the body. Abnormalities of the chromosomes, such as extra or missing chromosomal material, may affect the way the brain is formed and the way it functions.

To examine the chromosomes, a small amount of blood is collected and cultured for a few days in the laboratory. The blood sample is then processed and stained with dye so that the chromosomes can be seen under the microscope.

Abnormalities of the chromosomes are so infrequently found in children with learning difficulties who are of normal intelligence that this test is only performed if the paediatrician finds some indication from the history or physical examination that a chromosomal abnormality is likely to be present.

Electroencephalogram (EEG)

This is a test where the electrical activity normally present in the brain is measured. A special fabric cap is placed on the child's head. The cap has wires connected to a machine that records the brain's electricity in the form of a tracing on paper.

An EEG is a useful test if it is suspected that the child is performing poorly at school because of 'petit mal' epilepsy. This is a condition characterized by repeated episodes where the child goes blank for a moment, and so misses what is being said. Although petit mal epilepsy is often thought of, it is a very rare cause of learning difficulty. Most children who have blank episodes are simply day-dreaming, or voluntarily ignoring something they do not want to hear.

The paediatrician will arrange an EEG if he or she thinks that the story is suggestive of petit mal epilepsy. In other cases of children with learning difficulties, the EEG is generally unhelpful. Slightly abnormal tracings on EEG are quite common and of no practical importance.

Cognitive event-related potentials

These are a series of measurements obtained when an EEG machine, connected to a special computer, records electrical responses in the brain when specific tasks are undertaken. For example, when asked to listen for a sound, a child must allocate attention, and an event-related potential recorded when the child attends to the sound will contain elements that reflect the process of deployment of attentional capacity that takes place in the brain.

When children with certain types of specific learning difficulty concentrate intently on a sound, they do not generate the same strong waves that normal children do. This can be detected by measuring their cognitve event-related potentials.

The usefulness of this test is that it provides objective evidence of certain brain immaturities and inefficiencies. It cannot be used in isolation, but forms part of the information that is required to determine the nature of a child's learning difficulties.

Skull X-ray

Skull X-rays will generally not show any abnormality in a child with a learning difficulty and are not routinely done on such children. They should only be performed if the paediatrician suspects one of the rare conditions associated with learning difficulties where there may be abnormal findings on the skull X-ray.

Computerized axial tomography (CAT scan) and magnetic resonance imaging (MRI scan)

Both of these tests provide a detailed, computerized picture of the structure of the brain. The CAT scan picture is formed with the use of X-rays, while the MRI scan uses magnetic fields. Neither test will show an abnormality in the vast majority of children with learning difficulties. They are only performed if the paediatrician has reason to suspect that one of a group of uncommon conditions may be present.

Explanation of the findings to the parents

Both the psychologist and the paediatrician will provide a thorough explanation of their findings shortly after they have examined the child. It is well known that parents have difficulty remembering everything that they are told at an assessment, and often forget to ask questions. If you do not understand any aspect of the explanation, do not hesitate to ask questions at the end of the assessment, or to phone later with questions that occur to you.

You should also request that a copy of the assessment report be sent to you. It is a good idea to start a file in which all copies of reports pertaining to your child can be kept in chronological order. Such a file may be useful for professionals who see your child in the future.

Recommendation of an appropriate management plan

Having discussed the results of the assessment, the psychologist and paediatrician will be able to make recommendations about ways of helping your child. Remember that these are only suggestions: you know your child and family best, and will need to decide whether you feel that the recommendations are right for your child and your family. If you are unhappy with any of the suggestions, do not hesitate to tell the psychologist and paediatrician so that alternative strategies can be found.

It is usually beneficial if the psychologist or paediatrician speaks to your child's teacher after the assessment. This allows discussion of the recommendations to ensure that they fit in with the school's programme.

Review assessments

If a child's problems resolve, reassessment will not be needed; however, if the child continues to have difficulties, further assessments should be carried out to monitor the child's progress and ensure that his special needs are met. The interval between assessments is a matter for individual decision by the psychologist and paediatrician.

Psychologists cannot administer the same test to a child too frequently, as this enables him to learn how to do some of the tasks and so invalidates the result. Most tests cannot be repeated in less than 12 months.

Reviews may not always entail formal retesting, but may simply provide an opportunity to discuss how things are progressing. A report from the child's teacher should be requested for all reviews.

3 Theories of causation

Teach thy tongue to say, 'I do not know'.
Maimonides, physician and philosopher (1135–1204)

In the definition of specific learning difficulties in the first chapter I emphasized that the delay in learning must be 'unexplained'. It is, therefore, explicit in the definition that the cause of specific learning difficulties is presently unknown.

There are few things more frustrating for a doctor to say, or for a parent to hear, than that the cause of a child's condition is unknown. There is a natural tendency in such situations to alleviate this discomfort by guessing the cause. This is not necessarily bad, as it is by developing theories and devising experiments to test them that our knowledge advances. But the danger is that in our desire to know the cause with certainty, we may come to believe in a theory so strongly that we think of it as a fact.

Theories about specific learning difficulties abound. Most are based on the assumption that there is some impairment of brain function. These theories are not mutually exclusive, since each may explain one step in the chain of events that gives rise to specific learning difficulties, as shown in Figure 1. Let us look at these theories one by one.

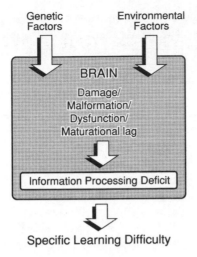

Figure 1. A chain of events that may lead to a specific learning difficulty.

Theories about the underlying cause

These theories attempt to explain the most fundamental aspect of the condition: its primary cause.

It is unlikely that a single factor can be responsible for a specific learning difficulty. Rather, it seems that a number of factors must act together. Such causation is known as 'multifactorial'.

There have been two groups of factors that have been suggested in the causation of specific learning difficulties: genetic factors and environmental factors.

Genetic factors

There is strong evidence for a genetic factor playing a role in the causation of specific learning difficulties. A number of studies have shown that children with specific learning difficulties are more likely to have a close relative with the same specific learning difficulty. No consistent pattern of inheritance has been described: sometimes it seems to be inherited from the mother, at other times from the father.

For all types of such learning difficulty, boys outnumber girls by about three to one. This vulnerability of boys suggests that genes carried on the X chromosome may play a part in many cases. As explained in the previous chapter, chromosomes are small, rod-like structures that carry the genes and are present in every cell of the body. Boys have only one X chromosome, which they inherit from their mothers, and a Y chromosome from their fathers; girls have two X chromosomes, one from each parent. If a boy inherits an X chromosome with a small defect that can cause a specific learning difficulty, he does not have another X chromosome to counteract its effect. A girl, on the other hand, would be protected by having the second, normal, X chromosome. Our knowledge of the genetics of specific learning difficulties suggests that, while genes on the X chromosome are important, other genes carried on other chromosomes probably also contribute to causation.

Another reason for suspecting that genetic factors play a role is that specific learning difficulties are more common in children with certain genetic syndromes, as was mentioned in the last chapter. In these cases, genetic factors would explain the higher frequency of specific learning difficulties in these children.

Environmental factors

There have been a number of studies to determine whether problems in pregnancy, labour, delivery, and the early newborn period are more common in children with specific learning difficulties. The results of these studies have been inconsistent: some have shown an association, while others have not. Some studies have found that clusters of problems are more likely to be associated with specific learning difficulties than single problems. Others have found that problems are more likely to lead to a specific learning difficulty when accompanied by socio-economic deprivation.

Some factors that may play a role prior to birth cannot be studied easily. For example, a pregnant woman may contract a viral infection during pregnancy that does not cause her ill-health, but is a factor in causing a specific learning difficulty in her child. Such illnesses would be very difficult to detect and so cannot be excluded as playing a role, on the basis of present data.

Adverse factors during infancy and later childhood have not been shown to be more common in children with specific learning difficulties. The way in which children are reared has also not been shown to relate to the development of specific learning difficulties.

Theories about brain damage, malformation, dysfunction, and maturation

Tests have failed to detect direct evidence of brain damage in children with specific learning difficulties. This has led to the formulation of theories about forms of undetectable abnormality in the brains of children with specific learning difficulties.

Undetectable brain damage theory

Some of the learning problems experienced by children with recognized brain damage are similar to those experienced by children with specific learning difficulties. For example, children who have a severe episode of viral encephalitis (viral inflammation of the brain) may be left with difficulties indistinguishable from those of a specific learning difficulty. A child who was a good reader before the illness may be unable to read after the illness, despite being unchanged in any other way. Another child may be affected by becoming overactive, impulsive, and distractable. Such changes can be associated with damage to parts of the brain that is demonstrable by CAT and MRI scans; but sometimes damage, although presumed to have occurred, cannot be detected on these tests. This raises the question of whether specific learning difficulties, too, may be a result of brain damage that is not detectable by present-day tests. We have no way of seeing individual nerve cells in the brain, except under the microscope. Small but significant areas of brain cell damage could go undetected by our tests.

Minor brain malformation theory

This is similar to the undetectable brain damage theory, but instead of proposing damage to the brain, it suggests that parts of the brain were malformed during fetal life. Such malformation would presumably involve the formation and distribution of nerve cells in such a way that the brain is less efficient in learning. The malformations would be so small that they could not be seen on CAT and MRI scans. This theory would fit in with the evidence for an underlying genetic cause, as it is the genes that control the way the brain is formed. There is, at present, no direct evidence that such minor malformations are present in children with specific learning difficulties.

Minimal brain dysfunction theory

The brain contains many natural chemicals, called neurotransmitters, that are involved in controlling its function by relaying messages from one nerve cell to another.

This theory explains specific learning difficulties on the basis of abnormalities in the nature or amount of these neurotransmitters. These disrupt the ability of the brain to learn. To describe such abnormal function, the term 'dysfunction' is used to differentiate it from damage and malformation. Such chemical abnormalities could be a result of genetic defects, since the synthesis of these substances in the brain is under genetic control.

A large amount of evidence points to neurotransmitter abnormalities as the basis for certain causes of short attention span in children (see Chapter 10). However, evidence for neurotransmitter abnormalities has not been found in other forms of learning difficulty.

Maturational lag theory

We know that as all children grow, they become more capable; but we do not know what changes in the brain are associated with this increased competence. The maturational lag theory proposes that areas of the brain of children with specific learning difficulties have not yet undergone these changes, and so the children are delayed in one or more areas of learning.

Critics of this theory point out that there is evidence that children with specific learning difficulties are not just delayed, but are different to other children in the way that they learn. In many cases it is impossible to determine whether the differences occur as a result of these children's difficulties with learning, or whether they are their cause. This debate about 'different versus delayed' has not yet been resolved.

Theory of cerebral dominance failure

This 'dominance failure' theory proposes that specific learning difficulties are due to failure of one side of the brain to become dominant over the other. This is a theory that is often too readily accepted by those who use terms such as 'cerebral dominance' and 'laterality' without realizing how difficult these are to ascertain, and how complex their interrelationship is.

The major part of the brain consists of two halves: the right and left cerebral hemispheres. They are connected by a bundle of nerve fibres called the corpus callosum. The two cerebral hemispheres have similar appearances and complementary functions. Each controls the movement of the opposite side of the body: the right hemisphere controls movement on the left side of the body and the left hemisphere controls movement on the right side. Usually one hemisphere has the area that controls most of the language function, while the other is more important for other functions such as spatial, complex visual, and musical skills. By convention we refer to the *cerebral hemisphere that controls language* as the 'dominant' hemisphere. This is because language is such an important function. Sometimes, but not always, this hemisphere is slightly larger than the non-dominant, or minor hemisphere.

Most people have a preference for their one hand that is stronger and more skilful than the other. This preference for one or other side is known as 'laterality'. In most right-handers, laterality and dominance correspond, i.e. their left cerebral hemisphere controls both language and the preferred hand. In some, though, their language may be controlled by their right hemisphere. This dominant hemisphere does not, in such cases, control the preferred hand.

By contrast, in most left-handers, dominance and laterality do not correspond; their language is usually controlled by their left cerebral hemisphere, while their preferred hand is controlled by their right. Some left-handers have language controlled by both areas.

The dominance failure theory states that one cerebral hemisphere has to dominate over the other, that is, become specialized in certain functions, notably language, in order for a child to be able to learn. If this does not occur, it will give rise to confusion and delay: the so-called 'strephosymbolis' (twisted signs), postulated by Dr Samuel T. Orton in 1925.

Two findings are usually quoted in support of the theory. First, there is evidence that children with specific learning difficulties are often late in developing hand preference, and second, there are reports of 'crossed laterality' in children with specific learning difficulties.

'Crossed laterality' is the term used for children who use limbs on different sides of their body for different actions: for example, their right hand to write, and their left to catch a ball. It is also used to describe other situations: for example, the preference for the left eye in a right-handed person, or the preference for the right foot in a left-hander.

There are important objections to the use of these data to support this theory. Tests for laterality, particularly foot, eye, and ear preference, are not reliable. Much of the information on laterality and learning is contradictory and there is a great variation in the relationship between laterality and dominance. In addition, laterality may have nothing to do with hemisphere dominance in many children. A child may prefer one eye, or one ear, because of some minor localized problem in the other, not because of cerebral hemispheric dominance.

The cerebral hemisphere dominance theory, therefore, remains unproved. Unfortunately, it has already given rise to much dubious testing of laterality and the implementation of teaching practices that are of questionable value. These will be discussed in Chapter 13.

Theory of information processing deficits

The brain is a computer that has been 'pre-wired' to learn. Information goes to the brain from the sense organs and is analysed and then stored in the memory for later recall, or is dealt with in some other way. These processes can be shown on a flowchart in the way that one can study the workings of a computer. Some workers have focused their attention on the particular problems experienced by children with specific learning difficulties, and have formulated theories about the precise deficits in information processing in their brains.

A model of the different steps involved in processing information is produced and hypotheses are put forward about where deficits could occur. Research studies are then designed to test these hypotheses. This field has provided great insights into specific learning difficulties over the last decade.

Figure 2 shows a simplified flowchart that illustrates the information processing that occurs when an adult reads aloud. A printed word is transmitted via the eyes to the brain, where it undergoes a number of steps. First, it is analysed to detect whether it is a familiar word or not. If familiar, it is processed along a lexical route (A). If the word is completely unrecognizable, it will be processed along a phonological route (B). The existence of these two different routes has now been established from clinical and research data.

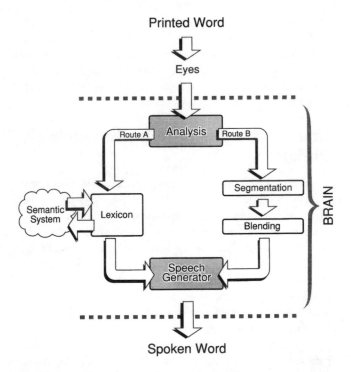

Figure 2. The reading process in the brain.

The first step on route A is for the word to enter a *lexicon*, or dictionary, which is connected to a *semantic system* where the meanings of all words already known by the individual are stored. Once the meaning is matched to the word, the word can be sounded by the speech generator, where the movements required to speak the word are initiated and controlled by the brain.

An unfamiliar word may be processed via route B. Here, the meaningless letters of the word are broken up into its component sounds (*phoneme segmentation*). Before the word can be spoken, the sounds must be joined back together (*phoneme blending*). Speech is then initiated by the speech generator in the same way as for a familiar word.

With this model in mind, one can check whether a child with specific reading difficulty has a deficit in lexical or phonological procedures. For example, is the child significantly better when reading actual words (lexical system) than nonsense words (phonological system)? If so, teaching may need to focus on ways to help the child develop his weak phonological skills.

It should be realized that children with specific learning difficulties are a heterogeneous group, and that the research findings in one group of children may not apply to all children with the disorder.

Another difficulty in interpreting data is the chicken or the egg problem: do the findings reflect the underlying cause of the difficulty, or are they the result of the difficulty? For example, because a child with specific reading difficulty cannot read well, he reads less and, therefore, has less reading experience to draw on than other children of his age. Some of the deficits in information processing that are regarded as a cause of specific reading difficulty may be the result of this lack of reading experience rather than a primary cause. For this reason, research data from studies that compare children with specific learning difficulties with other children of the same chronological age should be interpreted with caution. It may be more appropriate to compare such children with normal children of a younger age, who are at the same level of ability in the area being studied and at the same stage of learning.

A third important aspect of interpreting information processing data in children is the need to take into account so-called 'critical periods'. Certain methods of processing information in the brain may be required at certain stages of learning a skill such as reading. A process may be present when we test a child with established difficulties, and we may not realize that it was the absence of this very process, at some crucial stage in the past, that was responsible for the child's disorder. A developmental approach must, therefore, always be taken in interpreting information processing deficits in children.

4

How parents can help—general principles

This chapter provides general guidelines for helping a child with a specific learning difficulty. Advice on providing help in particular areas of learning is given in the next section of the book.

Parents of children with specific learning difficulties need information on how to teach their child and how to build up his self-esteem. In addition, they need help in coping with their own feelings and those of their other children. Let us look first at parents' concerns.

Parents' concerns

Parents of a child with specific learning difficulties often feel great anxiety about their child. They worry about how their child will cope at school, both academically and socially. They worry about how he will manage if teased, and if made to feel inadequate. When he gets home from school, they are sensitive to his feelings, saddened by his disappointments, and made anxious about his concerns.

Parents often feel guilty about their child's difficulties, wrongly imagining that they are somehow to blame. They may feel angry much of the time too: angry with teachers who fail to understand their child's problems, and angry with doctors who cannot explain their child's difficulties.

Many parents feel confused by the wide range of opinions about their child's condition and the variety of treatments that people suggest. They often wonder whether they are doing enough for their child, and whether there is something more they should be doing.

They may feel many other emotions as well. They may be embarrassed by their child's difficulties, hurt by other people's insensitive remarks, and overwhelmed by the task of teaching their child to overcome his difficulties.

There is no one right way to cope with these feelings; no single prescription that will work for all parents. Most parents do cope and do find that things become easier with time. Many find it helpful to have someone to share their feelings with: a friend, a spouse, or a professional; someone who will listen sympathetically and not be judgemental, or too quick to offer advice. Some parents obtain this support from meeting other parents of a child with a similar difficulty. You may be able to meet someone through one of the support groups for parents of children with specific learning difficulties. Some of these are listed in the Appendix of this book.

It is helpful to take one step at a time. Set yourself short-term, realistic goals and concentrate on them. Try to avoid looking too far ahead. After all, your child, you, and the opportunities available to you will all change in ways that cannot always be predicted.

Keeping active is another way of coping—not the frantic kind of busyness that gives you no repose, but doing constructive things that are both diverting and fulfilling.

Parents also need to develop strategies for coping with other people's hurtful remarks about their child. It is worthwhile giving some thought to this, so that you do not find yourself unprepared. First, you can try to set an example. If someone says something inappropriate, you can simply repeat what they have said in a more appropriate way. Some parents are helped by giving themselves silent pep-talks such as, 'This man doesn't know what he is talking about'. If you know that you are going to experience a difficult but unavoidable situation, it may be worth your while rehearsing the situation before it takes place. You may do this on your own or with someone close to you. You will probably decide on a series of responses that are more appropriate than those that would have occurred without rehearsal. Sometimes such responses can be used on subsequent occasions in similar situations. It is also important to provide information to those around you so that they understand your child's difficulties. It may be helpful to lend a book, such as this one, to a friend who does not understand your child's condition.

Siblings' needs

Parents need to be aware of the special pressures that their other children may face. These are their needs to understand the nature of the specific learning difficulty, to receive attention of their own from their parents, and to cope with the attitudes and comments of other children.

Siblings of a child with a specific learning difficulty need to understand that their brother or sister is not being lazy or naughty when he or she has difficulties with learning. They need to feel that they are not being discriminated against when their parents need to spend more time helping their brother or sister.

If a sibling is being teased about his brother or sister, it is important to acknowledge how hurt he must feel. Encourage him to express his anger and resentment and respond sympathetically. It is often difficult for a sibling to ignore unkind comments from his peers. It may help your child to imagine that he or she has a 'magnetic force field' surrounding his body that deflects any insults before they get to him. In this age of science fiction videos and movies, this idea often appeals to children. It may be beneficial to ask the teacher to provide some help too. Sometimes the teacher can initiate a discussion about 'being different' or 'having difficulties' that may change the attitudes of other children.

Building up your child's self-esteem

Children compare themselves with their peers from an early age. Children with specific learning difficulties soon realize that they face hurdles that other children do not. Many devise successful mechanisms for maintaining their self-esteem despite their difficulties; but some develop maladaptive mechanisms for coping. Parents can play an important role in building up their child's self-esteem.

Self-esteem is crucial for children with specific learning difficulties because it enables them to get into a cycle of success. If they have faith in their ability, they will try harder. If they try harder, they are more likely to succeed, thereby further increasing their feeling of self-worth. By contrast, low self-esteem can cause a vicious cycle of failure. The child tries to evade failure by avoiding challenges. This results in poor attainments that reinforce the child's feelings of inadequacy. Parents need to encourage their child to enter the cycle of success.

The development of self-esteem has important implications for the child's future. If a child has not attained good self-esteem by adulthood, he will derive little value from his academic skills. If he has good self-esteem, he will probably cope well with life, even if his academic ability is limited.

How can you, as parents, engender high self-esteem in your child with a specific learning difficulty? First, you should try to accept your child's weaknesses. He needs love that is not conditional upon his achievement. You also need to accept his feelings, without criticism.

Try to emphasize his positive attributes, and show how you value them. He needs plenty of praise for his efforts. Do not say 'Well done' or 'Good boy', but rather 'You spelt that difficult word very well', or 'That was excellent reading'. Make it clear what you are praising him for.

Children learn self-esteem from their parents' example. This is one of the reasons that children whose parents have high self-esteem are more likely to have high self-esteem themselves. You need to have faith in yourself. Let your child hear you praise your own accomplishments (for example, 'I'm very pleased with the way this cake has turned out', or 'That was a job well done').

Encourage your child to set realistic goals so that he can experience success. Most importantly, help him to evaluate his achievements realistically, so that he is not overly critical of himself. It is important to set achievable goals at the start of any activity. If your child is going to attempt something that is too difficult for him, guide him to a more suitable activity in a tactful way.

You should also teach your child to praise himself. If he achieves something, ask him, 'How do you think you did?', or 'Are you pleased with your spelling of these words now?'. Teach him also to praise others (for example, 'What do you think of dad's salad?').

Your child needs special time with you to feel loved. Special time does not mean that you have to organize activities away from home. It is time when you are able to give attention to your child in a way that builds up his self-esteem. The important thing is that it should be enjoyable for your child, and that he should be receiving your full attention.

Children also need to feel they belong to something. It may be an idea to arrange for your child to join a hobby group, a scout pack, or some other such unit. Encourage him to feel proud of his school, his neighbourhood, and his ethnic tradition.

Children need to feel they have the power to make some of the choices that affect their lives. Whenever possible, let him select things for himself, such as which clothes he wears, in what order he does things, and which books he takes from the library. Admire his choices and praise his self-sufficiency.

Another way of increasing your child's self-esteem is by enriching his experiences. Take him on excursions, teach him to do new things like gardening, or make a photo album with pictures of himself—all these things increase his feelings of self-worth. Give him opportunities to become self-reliant: teach him to make small purchases on his own, to answer the telephone, and to take responsibility for some household task.

Parents should be aware of some of the common defences that children develop to cope with feelings of low self-esteem, as these can easily be misinterpreted. If wrongly handled, the child's self-esteem may be further lowered. These defences include aggressive behaviour, withdrawal, and frequent quitting. Management of these, and other coping mechanisms, are discussed in Chapter 12.

Telling your child about his learning difficulty

It is a good idea to tell your child about his specific learning difficulty at an early stage. Do not wait until he becomes confused and discouraged. Explain that different people are talented in different ways. Point out those things at which he is better, and the special qualities he has. Tell him about the things that you find difficult. Then explain that some things are very difficult for him too, even when he tries very hard. Acknowledge how frustrating this must be for him, but also point out the special ways in which some of his difficulties are being overcome. You can also tell him the stories of people such as Thomas Alva Edison, Sir Winston Churchill, and Paul Elvström who had successful careers despite having experienced difficulties with their school work. You should be able to find suitable biographies of such people in the local children's library.

It is worthwhile bearing in mind that some children, once they know they have a specific learning difficulty, use this as an excuse for quitting. You can quickly eradicate this if, from the outset, you draw a clear distinction between difficulty and laziness. It is also beneficial if you always praise effort and not only results.

Parents as teachers

Parents have an important role in helping their child to learn. They teach by example, often without realizing it, as well as in a more direct way. For a child with a specific learning difficulty, the parent's role as teacher becomes even more important. No other teacher can spend as much one-to-one time with a child as a parent. No other teacher has the opportunity to extend what the child has learned in so many different situations. However, a child's relationship with his parent is generally so much more intense than that with any other teacher, that parents must approach teaching their child with care. Most parents can be good at teaching their child provided that they make this a positive and constructive experience for the child. This means that the parent must be prepared to put some thought into how to become an effective teacher.

Before you teach your child, you should liaise with his teacher. He or she will ensure that what you teach complements what is being done at school. A good teacher will be happy to give you guidance about what to teach and how to go about it. He or she will be only too aware that there is usually insufficient time to give adequate individual attention to each child in the class.

When you teach your child, do not overdo it. Short daily sessions are much better than infrequent long sessions. Attempt small units of work at a time.

Choose a time when you are both feeling calm. You need a quiet environment where you will not be disturbed. It might be necessary to arrange for your other children to be occupied somewhere else. Do not try to have a teaching session while you are doing something else, while the TV is on, or when siblings are around.

Try to make sessions as enjoyable and as varied as possible. Start with revision of previous work, and explain what you hope to achieve in this session and why it is important. Work slowly and patiently. Sometimes your child will seem to have a block, or forget things that he knew the previous day. Take this in your stride. It is perfectly normal for children to progress at a slow rate, with sudden spurts followed by protected periods of little progress. During these slow phases, children are consolidating skills before going on to the next stage.

Always be encouraging, never critical. Avoid expressions such as 'Hurry up', 'Watch what you're doing', 'Don't be careless', and 'You've seen that word before'. Instead, use phrases such as 'You're really improving at reading' and 'You really worked hard on it'. Note that the praise should, whenever possible, make it clear what you are praising. Praise effort, not just achievement.

There are many ways of rewarding good effort. The simplest sort of reward would be to praise what the child has done by making a fuss and saying 'Good spelling', and so on. These simple verbal rewards should always be given, and are often more powerful than parents realize. This sort of reward is usually enough but in some children it may be necessary to institute a tangible reward system. This may take the form of a star on a chart, or a 'smiley' stamp on the hand. In more sophisticated children, it may be necessary to have a system where a specific number of small tokens earns something a little larger. Beware of the trap of making the reward too expensive. You should not make it too easy to get big rewards, although you should make it reasonably easy to earn lesser rewards to encourage your child. The reward system should be carefully planned before it is explained to him. Stamps, tokens, or charts should be available at the outset.

Whenever you have a teaching session with your child, try to end it with an activity that he is good at and enjoys. At the end, do not forget to say something like 'That was fun, I look forward to doing some more with you tomorrow'.

When the session is over, try to stop playing the part of the teacher. You are more than a teacher, you are a parent as well. Parents cannot treat every interaction with their child as an opportunity for teaching without the relationship becoming stilted and the child becoming resentful. There must be opportunities for unstructured interaction.

Teaching has to concentrate on a child's areas of weakness. Most children are aware from an early age of the things they find difficult. Like the rest of us, they tend to want to do the things they are better at. Make certain that you give your child ample opportunities to do those things he is good at, in addition to those he finds difficult. This is essential for his self-confidence.

Some parents do not have the time, or the ability, to teach their child. If this is the case, it is usually best to find a teacher or coach to help your child after school. It is important to choose someone with the skills and temperament to do this well. Support organizations often have lists of suitable teachers. The names of some of these organizations can be found in the Appendix.

Working with the school

It is best to regard yourself, the teachers, and the other professionals (such as a speech therapist) involved in your child's education as a team. Each member of the team plays a part in providing the best education for your child. It is essential that you and the other members of the team communicate regularly.

Some schools have a file for each child which is passed on to their new teacher each year. Do not rely on this, but arrange a meeting with your child's new teacher at the beginning of each year. At the meeting, explain your child's difficulties and give the teacher copies of any assessments done in the past.

During the year, keep in regular contact with the teacher to find out how your child is progressing. It is a good idea for your child's homework diary to be used as a 'communication book' in which you and the teacher can exchange information on a regular basis. You should not hesitate to request a special meeting with your child's teacher if there is something that is causing you concern. Do this as early as possible.

In some places it is possible to apply for funding for special teaching sessions at school for a child with a specific learning difficulty. This may be given in the class, or in a resource room. The child may receive individual help, or be part of a small group of children with similar difficulties. If you think this may be helpful, check with your child's teacher to see whether it is available. Some schools also have an arrangement whereby parents come to the class and help children with their reading, or other work.

Help from organizations

There are now a number of organizations that provide support to parents of children with specific learning difficulties. Such associations vary in their activities. They generally produce a newsletter, run a library, and sell books of interest to parents. Some have meetings where parents can share experiences. They also lobby governments for better services for children with specific learning difficulties. There is usually an annual membership fee.

Part 2
Areas of learning

5 Reading

When the English tongue we speak
Why is 'break' not rhymed with 'freak'
Will you tell me why it's true
We say 'sew' but likewise 'few'?
And the maker of a verse
Cannot cap his 'horse' with 'worse'
'Beard' sounds not the same as 'heard',
'Cord' is different from 'word'.
'Cow' is 'cow', but 'low' is 'low',
'Shoe' is never rhymed with 'roe'.
Think of 'hose' and 'dose' and 'lose'
And think of 'goose' and yet of 'choose'.
Think of 'comb' and 'tomb' and 'bomb',
'Doll' and 'roll', and 'home' and 'come'.
And since 'pay' is rhymed with 'say',
Why not 'paid' with 'said', pray?
We have 'blood' and 'food' and 'good',
'Mould' is not pronounced like 'could'.
Wherefore 'done', but 'gone' and 'lone'
Is there any reason known?
And, in short, it seems to me,
Sounds and letters disagree!

Anonymous

Specific reading difficulty is the best known, and best studied, form of specific learning difficulty. This is the condition that many refer to as 'dyslexia'.

We will define specific reading difficulty as a significant, unexplained delay[1] in reading in a child of average, or above average, intelligence. Specific reading difficulty is, therefore, a form of specific learning difficulty where reading is the particular learning skill affected. Other forms of specific learning difficulty may also be present, particularly spelling, writing, and spoken language difficulties.

It should be noted that the diagnosis of specific reading difficulty is based on the degree of delay in reading, rather than on the particular type of errors that the child makes. Much has been made of certain characteristics of children's reading, such as difficulty in distinguishing 'b' from 'd', reluctance to read aloud, a monotonous voice when reading, and a tendency to follow the text with the finger when reading. There is nothing diagnostic about these characteristics. They are seen in many children when they first start learning to read (and some are seen in adults when they learn to read a foreign language). The diagnosis of specific reading difficulty should only be made after a comprehensive assessment of intellectual and reading ability, and an exclusion of other causes of poor reading attainment (see Chapter 2).

How common is specific reading difficulty?

The best evidence for the existence of specific reading difficulty as an entity is given by the results of a study by Professor Michael Rutter and his colleagues, who tested 9–10-year-olds on the Isle of Wight. They first tested the children to determine their intelligence and reading ability. They then studied all the children whose reading was significantly behind that of their peers and found that

---

[1] A significant delay is usually defined as a reading level *more than two standard deviations below the mean* for the child's age (see footnote on p. 6 for the explanation of this term).

these could be divided into two groups: those where the delayed reading could be explained by low intelligence and a second group where the children were of normal intelligence and the reading difficulty could not be explained. This latter group fits our definition of specific reading difficulty.

The researchers found that there were more children in this specific reading difficulty group than would be anticipated if they just represented the lower end of a nominal variation in reading ability. There was an unexpected 'hump' on the population frequency graph, suggesting that these children had a specific disorder causing their difficulties.[2] This was further suggested by a number of characteristics of these children.

- There were over three times as many boys in the group as girls.

- Speech and language problems were three times more common than in the rest of the population.

- A family history of similar difficulties in reading and speech was also three times as common as in the rest of the population.

- The children were more likely than other children to have difficulty discriminating right from left.

By contrast, the children in the group who were slow in their reading on the basis of low intelligence, were different in a number of ways from the children with specific reading difficulty: boys and girls were equally represented, an underlying cause of their problem was apparent in over 10 per cent, and mild abnormalities of movement were often found.

---

[2] The existence of this 'hump' is controversial. A study of children in Connecticut failed to show a 'hump'. Whether this is due to differences in methodology, or differences in the environment or genetic make-up of the children, is presently unknown.

In the Isle of Wight study, over three per cent of the children had specific reading difficulty, as we have defined it. A number of other studies have suggested that specific reading difficulty is more common than this in many other parts of the world. Commonly quoted figures range from three to ten per cent.

What competent reading involves

Reading is a complex process. Let us stop and consider what is involved as you, a competent reader, read this line aloud.

First, you must be motivated to read it, otherwise you would not bother. Secondly, you must be able to focus your attention on the text, undistracted by what is going on around you or by other thoughts. Then you must clearly see the shapes of the letters so that they can be transmitted to your brain. You must be able to let your eyes scan the letters from left to right, while at the same time breaking up the string of letters into words, words into phrases, and phrases into sentences. The shapes of the letters you see must be transmitted in sequence to the brain, their exact position in space retained. This is crucial: a picture of a cat remains a cat whether it is upside-down or on its side—a 'p' upside down is not a 'p' any more, it is a 'd'. Your brain must be able to recognize letters even if they are printed in an unusual typeface, in capitals, or in italics.

As a competent reader, the process that takes place in your brain as you read is an automatic one. You have an in-built store of words in your brain, known as a 'lexicon', that recognizes familiar words. Even unfamiliar words are generally decoded by your lexicon. This is done by a process of 'lexical analogy', where the lexicon searches for a familiar word on which to base the pronunciation of the unfamiliar word. The context in which the unfamiliar word is found will also influence its pronunciation.

This introduces us to the other important aspect of reading: comprehension. The lexicon is connected to a kind of dictionary in the brain, known as a 'semantic system'. This stores the meaning of all the words you know and allows all known words to be matched to their meanings.

Throughout this process you will need to remember the meanings of the words you have read so that you do not forget the first words of the paragraph by the time you reach the end. The meaning of sentences will also need to be remembered from page to page for the text to be understood.

Is this all? No, we still have not spoken about how your brain will imbue your reading out aloud with expression, different accents, and variations in volume and pitch; all of these require access to other parts of the brain where learned information is stored. And all these processes are carried out simultaneously, and with lightning speed!

How reading is learned

The description above deals with the competent reader. The subject of how this skill is acquired by a child is even more complicated.

As we have seen, competent reading relies on an in built lexicon that can recognize familiar words. When an individual has a well-furnished lexicon and can use this for word recognition, he is at the *automatic* (or orthographic) stage of reading. Most normal children do not reach this stage until eight to ten years of age. After this, they continue to improve the efficiency of their reading, but the processes involved remain the same.

How does a child reach this stage? We have only recently begun to understand this. Children need to go through two preparatory stages before they can reach the stage of automatic reading.

The first stage is the *visual memory* (or logographic) stage. This does not involve the lexical system (the lexicon is empty). Instead, words are recognized as if they were familiar people or objects. For example, the word 'Bill' is short and has two little 'sticks' on the right. 'Help!' may be recognized simply by its exclamation mark (and therefore 'Bang!' may be read as 'Help!' at this stage).

Eventually, this system must be superseded. Many words are too similar in shape and length for a purely visual recognition system to differentiate between them. In addition, spelling cannot advance beyond a very rudimentary stage if visual recognition alone is relied upon.

The next, very important stage, is the *phonological* (or alphabetic) stage. Normal children usually enter this stage at six to seven years. At this stage, children bring into play a special system for reading that is essential if they are to furnish their lexicon so that they can progress to the automatic stage. The system used is an alternative pathway to the lexical system. It is called the phonological system, because words are broken down (segmented) into their component sounds (*phonos* means sound).

The smallest units of sound are called 'phonemes'. The English language has 44 different phonemes. There are only 26 letters in the alphabet, so some phonemes are represented by combinations of letters (for example, 'ai' in 'rain'). Any letter, or group of letters, that corresponds to a phoneme is called a 'grapheme'. As the poem at the beginning of this chapter illustrates, the same group of letters (graphemes) may correspond to different phonemes, depending on the word. This reflects the complex history of the evolution of written English.

Phonological reading is, therefore, not just a simple one-to-one matching process; knowing the correct phoneme means that the brain must learn the 577 grapheme-to-phoneme correspondences in the English language. It must learn to look at the word as a whole and evaluate the letters in the light of learned rules about phonemes. Sometimes, in order to know which phoneme is appropriate, the context in which the word is used must be taken into account. As children acquire more ability to translate the graphemes they see on the page into the correct phonemes, they start filling their brain's lexicon with words. When this happens, they can start bypassing the phonological system and access the lexicon whenever they read a familiar word. Soon, they rarely use the relatively slow phonological system, and are reading automatically like an adult.

At one time it was not realized that children had to go through this phonological stage, because in the normal child this stage is not obvious. Although they are reading by 'sound' rather than by 'sight', they do not actually need to sound the words out. The phoneme segmentation and recombination occur in the brain, silently and rapidly.

The deficit in specific reading difficulty

As we have seen, children require phonological skills to furnish their lexicon during the second stage of learning to read. If they do not have these skills, automatic reading does not seem to be able to develop.

There have been many studies to try to pin-point the precise deficit in children with specific reading difficulty. Although such children represent a heterogeneous group, most children studied have been shown to have difficulties primarily with phonological skills. The most common area of difficulty is in *phoneme segmentation*, the process by which an unfamiliar word is broken up by the brain into its component sounds. It would seem that such children have problems cracking the code for converting graphemes into their corresponding phonemes in the brain. It is difficult for such children to progress through the phonological stage of reading and eventually, to become automatic readers. They may compensate for their phonological difficulties by trying to develop visual recognition techniques, but these are not usually sufficient for efficient reading. Often such children also have a *verbal memory* deficit, a difficulty recalling words that have just been read. This may further compound their problem.

Although most recent studies have shown phonological processing deficits to be the commonest cause of specific reading difficulty, not all children with this condition have this particular problem. Some children have difficulty in the way in which their brain perceives the shapes of letters, a *visual perception* deficit. The brains of such children are not good at recognizing or interpreting the shapes of letters on the page. This might be why children with specific reading difficulty often confuse letters such as 'b' and 'd'. Some children have mixed phonological and visual perception difficulties. As we shall see in the next chapter, children with phonological deficits are more likely to make phonetic errors in spelling, while children with visual perception problems are more likely to make visual errors.

How reading is assessed

There are a number of reading tests available to psychologists and teachers. Usually the child will be asked to read aloud from portions of text that have been graded according to difficulty. Easier texts have few, simple words in large print, often with illustrations. The child will progress to more and more difficult levels until it is clear to the tester that he has reached his upper limit.

The tests usually determine the child's *reading speed* relative to other children of his age. The number of errors the child makes are also noted to establish *reading accuracy*, which is also compared with age standards. After each portion of text has been read, the tester may ask the child a number of standard questions about what he has just read to determine the child's *reading comprehension*. This too can be compared with age standards.

Reading speed, accuracy, and comprehension can all be expressed in age levels. For example, a child of 8 years 4 months may have an accuracy reading age of 6 years

5 months, if he makes the same number of mistakes as the average child aged 6 years 5 months; and a comprehension reading age of 5 years 7 months, if he understands what he has read as well as an average child of 5 years 7 months.

In addition to these scores, the tester takes an interest in the particular types of error that the child makes. He or she may also give the child some specific tests to try to establish the exact nature of the reading problem. For example, he or she may test the child's visual perception: the brain's ability to make sense of what the eye sees. The tester may compare the child's ability to read real and nonsense words to evaluate his phonological skill.

Language and reading are closely related functions. Language difficulties are often present in children with reading difficulties, although they may be subtle and difficult to detect. For this reason, all children with reading difficulty should ideally have their language skills assessed by a speech therapist. Some may benefit from speech therapy.

How reading is taught

There are several different methods of teaching children to read. All have their advocates, and all have been successful in some children. Many teachers use a combination of methods, and may adopt the method that seems to suit the child best. Some schools use only one method for all children. I shall describe the common methods before discussing their individual merits for children with specific reading difficulty.

'Look and say' method

This is a popular method, where the child is introduced to a series of illustrated graded readers that have a limited number of simple, common ('key') words used over and over again. The child learns to recognize these words by sight and slowly expands his reading vocabulary.

Children using this scheme usually pick up the rules of decoding grapheme–phoneme correspondences on their own. Sometimes, children are encouraged to use the basic phonic method described below when they come across an unfamiliar word.

Phonic method

Basic phonics

In this method, the child is taught the sounds of letters and then encouraged to blend these into a word (for example, dog = d/o/g). The child then adds the word to his list of words. With experience, he learns to decode more complex grapheme–phoneme correspondences on his own.

Linguistic (or phonetic) method

Here the grapheme–phoneme correspondences are taught in a very organized way, starting with individual letter sounds and progressing to families of words that have the same sound. This method deals with all the different spelling patterns in a systematic way until words can be broken into 'chunks' (such as 'ar', 'tion', and 'ead'), which the child learns to recognize.

Embellished alphabet

These methods involve altering the traditional alphabet to make it easier for children to learn to read. An example of this is the i.t.a. (initial teaching alphabet), which is shown in Figure 3. Other such methods include the REBUS System and the DISTAR Reading System.

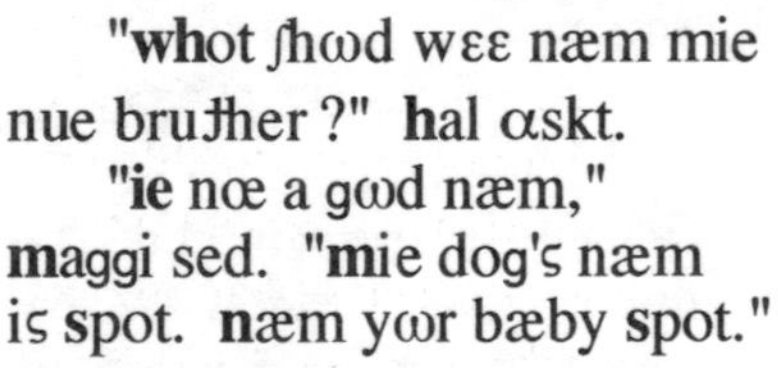

> "whot ʃhωd wεε næm mie
> nue bruθher ?" hal ɑskt.
> "ie nœ a gωd næm,"
> maggi sed. "mie dog'ʃ næm
> iʃ spot. næm yωr bæby spot."

Figure 3. An example of text written in the initial teaching alphabet (i.t.a.).

Language experience method

This is a method that utilizes the child's own language for his reading material, rather than a printed reader. For example, the child might tell the teacher a story which he or she writes down and then teaches the child to read.

Multisensory method

These are sometimes referred to as V–A–K–T (visual–auditory– kinaesthetic–tactile) techniques. They involve more than just looking at the letters. Other senses are brought into play: the child listens to the sound, feels the movement by tracing the letters (often with his eyes closed), and may also be given an opportunity to feel a three-dimensional model of the letter. Multisensory methods often involve the introduction of writing together with reading, so that tracing the letters can also be accomplished.

Teaching a child with specific reading difficulty to read

The first step in teaching a child with specific reading difficulty to read is to recognize that he has special problems. A study at three centres in England demonstrated that children who were identified as having specific reading difficulty improved dramatically once they received appropriate help. These children gained an average of nearly two years of reading progress over a one-year period, compared with six months progress per year before this.

Each child must be individually assessed and the assessment team, in conjunction with the child's teacher, should plan a method that suits the child best.

Most children with specific learning difficulty have great difficulties with phonological skills—they are unable to pick up phonological skills with the same natural ease as other children. Reading methods that do not approach these skills in an organized way are, therefore, generally inappropriate for children with specific reading difficulty. The 'Look and say' and language experience methods rely on the good phonological skills of ordinary children, and are not appropriate for children in whom such skills are lacking. Even the basic phonic method may not approach phonological skills in a way that is structured enough for many children with specific reading difficulty. The embellished alphabets mean that the child will have to learn the proper alphabet later, which may confuse him and add to his problems.

There is, therefore, general agreement that for most children with specific reading difficulty, a carefully structured linguistic (phonetic) scheme works best. Examples of two such schemes are the Alpha-to-Omega scheme and the Orton–Gillingham–Stillman method. These schemes teach reading and spelling together. They avoid whole words initially; they teach sounds first and work up to chunks of words. They emphasize the need to revise continually what the child has learned, to compensate for the poor retention of many children with specific reading difficulty.

Whichever method is used, a flexible approach should be adopted, with regular practice of the skills being taught.

How parents can help their child with specific reading difficulty

Every child with specific reading difficulty should have a careful assessment of his abilities and needs and have a teacher who understands these and plans educational strategies accordingly.

Class teachers usually do not have enough time to give every child in the class the supervision they need when reading. It is therefore essential that children have some supervised reading practice out of school hours. Some parents may be able to pay a teacher to do this regularly, but many will need to do it themselves.

Parents can play a major role in augmenting their child's reading programme. Discuss this with your child's teacher, so that you know how to help your child, and provide practice that is consistent with the programme at school. Here are some general guidelines on how you can help your child, to be used in conjunction with the advice about teaching and self-esteem in Chapter 4.

1. Choose a time for reading practice when you are both in a good frame of mind. Try to avoid having a practice session if you or your child are hungry, tired, or irritable. Make certain that other members of the family know not to disturb you.

2. It is best if you use a book that the teacher selects. If your child does not like the books he brings from school, as is often the case, discuss this with the teacher. If you are choosing the books yourself, ensure that the vocabulary used is suitable for your child's level of progress and that the print is clear. The easiest print to read is serif typeface (see Figure 4). Books with pictures are usually best. Do not worry if the child uses the pictures to guess the text. The main thing is that it is enjoyable and he is getting reading practice.

3. Make sure the child is comfortable and that there is good lighting. It is usually best if the child sits at a table with you on his right-hand side (unless you are left-handed).

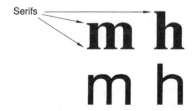

Figure 4. Serif (above) and sans-serif (below) typeface.

4. Start by looking at the cover of the book and discuss what the book may be about for a short while, then open it and let the child begin to read.

5. Encourage your child to follow the words with his finger, or with a pencil placed horizontally below the line he is reading. Later he can dispense with these aids.

6. Sometimes it is a good idea to share the reading, you and the child reading alternate pages. This is good for the child's self-esteem as he feels under less pressure, and helps you cover more of the story in a long book. The child will learn from following the print while you read your section.

7. *Paired reading* is another technique that may decrease tension between you and your child during reading practice. Your child's teacher may ask you to practise reading in this way, or you may suggest it to the teacher. In this method, parent and child read aloud in unison. You should follow the text with your finger and take care not to read too quickly, so that your child does not have difficulty keeping up. If your child wants to read alone at any stage, he gives you a prearranged signal and you then stop while he continues on his own. If the child runs into difficulties he can give a signal for you to join in again. The usual signals are a tap on the book, or a gentle nudge.

8. Do not try to cover too much, particularly in the early sessions. At first, a five-minute session is enough; this can then be increased to 10 or 15 minutes. Cut a session short if your child seems to be tiring. Aim for daily sessions.

9. If your child misreads a word that does not affect the meaning of the text, ignore it. If he misreads a word that affects the meaning of the text, wait for a natural break in

the text (the end of a sentence or paragraph) and say something like 'Wait a second, that did not quite make sense, did it?' or 'What is this word again?', and then encourage him to go back and check the word. If your child hesitates over an unfamiliar word, wait for a short time to see if he can manage to read it. If he has trouble, you may encourage him to sound it out, but if this does not help, read it clearly and slowly for him. Do not forget to praise him for his effort.

10. If there is an interruption, get your child to re-read from the beginning of the sentence, so that the flow of meaning is restored.

11. Do not worry if your child's reading is monotonous. Let him read with as much or as little expression as he wants. When children are struggling to read, they cannot give attention to reading with expression; that comes later.

12. At the end of the reading, discuss the book with him. Ask for his opinion about the story. It may be a good idea to go through the book page by page and look at the pictures while you talk.

13. Avoid negative comments. Do not make comments like 'Look what you're doing' and 'Concentrate, you got it right before'. Do make comments like 'Good reading' and 'You pronounced that difficult word clearly, well done!'.

14. Keep reading to your child at other times. Do not feel that because he is reading you should no longer read him stories, or let him listen to story tapes. These will only increase his enjoyment of books and stories, particularly since they will be more age-appropriate than those that he can read himself. Anything that encourages enjoyment of literature will be beneficial.

15. In older children with specific reading difficulty, it should be realized that their poor reading may deprive them of exposure to information that other children of their age have access to. This can be compensated for by reading books to the child that he is not yet able to read to himself.

16. You can help your child with his reading by playing games with him, as well as by listening to him read. Games like 'Snap' and 'Snakes and ladders' can be adapted so that reading is involved. 'Snap' cards can be made with words that match corresponding pictures, and 'Snakes and ladders' can be played with cards on which words are written instead of a dice; if the word is read correctly the player moves by the number of letters in the word. It is important that these games are played with a sense of fun.

Spelling

There are three kinds of difficulty that may cause a child's written work to be incomprehensible. First, specific spelling difficulty, where some words may be so badly spelt that they are difficult to recognize (Figure 5). Secondly, specific writing difficulty, where the handwriting may be so untidy that it is illegible (see Figure 10, p. 83). And, thirdly, language disorder, where the language used by the child may be so full of errors that it does not make sense (see Figure 23, p. 106).

Specific spelling difficulty will be described in this chapter, specific writing difficulty in the next chapter, and language disorders will be described in Chapter 9.

What is specific spelling difficulty?

Specific spelling difficulty can be defined as an unexplained, significant spelling difficulty. A significant

Las holiday I went wlth my bruther tho viset my annt on her fam. We sor many anemels. The best was the bobl He was very angree.

Figure 5. Specific spelling difficulty (12-year-old boy).

difficulty is usually defined as a spelling age *more than two standard deviations below the mean* for the child's age (see footnote on p. 6 for the explanation of this term).

Specific spelling difficulty is often associated with specific reading difficulty. In some children, specific spelling difficulty is an isolated problem. Although such children will have average reading ability, research studies suggest that subtle reading problems can be detected in such children on special testing.

How spelling is assessed

There are several standardized spelling tests in general use. These differ in the ways in which they test spelling. Some present the child with words that are part of his sight vocabulary, others present a wider range of words. Tests usually involve spelling from dictation. Some may also involve recognizing whether a printed word is correctly spelt or not.

The psychologist will choose the test, or tests, that will provide information about the child's spelling level, as well as about the nature of his difficulties. For example, a test that shows that a child has difficulties with spelling from dictation, but not with identifying words that are incorrectly spelt, may demonstrate particular problems with word memory. The psychologist will also try to differentiate between the different kinds of spelling errors, such as phonetic, visual, and sequential errors, which are described below.

The psychologist may also do other tests to establish the nature of the child's spelling difficulties. For example, if the child's spelling shows many phonetic errors, he or she might test the child's auditory discrimination skills, to assess whether he is able to distinguish between the different sounds he hears.

All children with specific spelling difficulty should have their hearing tested, as some spelling difficulties may be related to hearing impairment.

The deficit in specific spelling difficulty

Reading and writing are opposite processes. In reading, printed symbols (graphemes) are converted into their corresponding sounds (phonemes); in writing, phonemes are converted into their corresponding graphemes.

Spelling in the English language requires knowledge of the inconsistent rules for converting phonemes into the appropriate graphemes. The poem at the beginning of the previous chapter (p. 55) demonstrated how variable these rules are. A particular phoneme may be represented by different graphemes (for example, sn*uff* and en*ough*), and the same grapheme may correspond to different phonemes (for example en*ough*, hicc*ough*, and c*ough*). Words with the same phoneme, but different graphemes, are called homophones (for example, shoot and shute).

Correct spelling is not usually possible until the child reaches the phonological stage (which was described in the last chapter). It is only at this stage that awareness of grapheme–phoneme correspondence begins. There is some evidence that children enter this phase earlier for reading than writing.

It has been postulated that the spelling process consists of the steps shown in Figure 6. The word is first thought of in a part of the brain (*cognitive system*), and needs to enter a *graphemic buffer*, which will control the way it is spelt when written.

There are two different paths that the process can follow from the cognitive system to the graphemic buffer. If the word is familiar, it follows route A, if it is unfamiliar, route B must be followed.

Route A, for familiar words, involves matching the word to a store of words whose spelling is already known. This is a dictionary or 'lexicon' system, analogous to that used when familiar words are read.

Route B, for unfamiliar words, involves a phonological system where the word is broken down into its component

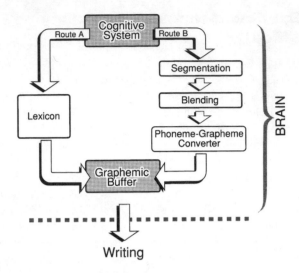

Figure 6. The spelling process in the brain.

sounds (phonemes), which are then processed by a phoneme-to-grapheme converter, prior to entering the graphemic buffer. The buffer controls the way the word is written down.

Once we see a word we have written down, after processing it through route B, we may realize that we have seen it before: we can then process it again, this time through route A, and correct it. This is probably the reason that we find it easier to spell words if we write them down first.

There is evidence that children with isolated spelling difficulty differ from children with combined reading and spelling difficulty on tests that identify the underlying cognitive deficit. Studies show that children with isolated spelling defects have relatively better language skills and that their difficulties lie in the phonological pathway (route B). Children with combined reading and specific spelling difficulty seem to have weaker language skills and have phonetic (phonological), as well as non-phonetic (lexical), deficits in spelling (routes A and B).

Spelling errors

It is possible to divide the errors made by children with specific spelling difficulty into a number of types. There is more than one process that may be involved in producing each type of spelling error, and so one must be careful not to regard each type of error as indicative of only one type of defect. For example, so-called 'phonetic errors' may be a result of problems with phoneme-to-grapheme conversion, but may also be owing to the child not attending to sounds, or not being able to discriminate between the different sounds he hears.

It should also be noted that individual children with specific spelling difficulty often show a combination of these errors, and that many show inconsistency in their errors from one moment to the next.

Nevertheless, if used in conjunction with careful assessment, identification of the type of error may be a useful guide to finding appropriate ways of helping a child with specific spelling difficulty.

Phonetic errors

These errors are very common in children with specific spelling difficulty. Phonetic errors will have some visual resemblance to the correct spelling, but sound different when read. For example, the child may write 'lap' for 'lip', or 'goase' for 'goose'. These errors suggest that the phonological system is not functioning properly. Such children often have difficulties with reading because of this impairment.

Visual errors

In contrast to phonetic errors, these sound correct, but look wrong. Examples are 'lite' for 'light' and 'grate' for 'great'. These errors suggest that the phonological system is being relied upon, because of difficulty with visual recall of familiar words (that is, a deficit in the lexical system described earlier).

Letter substitution errors

These errors result in the child writing 'pig' for 'big' or 'log' for 'dog'. They may be a result of hearing, or auditory discrimination, problems. They may also be caused by visual perception difficulties. These underlying causes may be differentiated by special testing.

Insertion and omission errors

In an insertion error, an extra letter is added to a word, for example 'beflore' for 'before'. In omission errors, letters are missing, such as 'bicyle' for 'bicycle'. These errors can be due to lexical or phonological problems. Some omissions, particularly those of soft, high-frequency sounds such as 'th', may be due to subtle hearing problems.

Sequential errors

Sequential confusion results in errors such as 'brigde' for 'bridge'. These are related to problems of sequential organization (see Chapter 10).

'Irrational' errors

These are errors that do not fit into the patterns described above. They neither look right nor sound right. Examples of such errors are 'ritt' for 'right' and 'lift' for 'laugh'. Careful analysis of some of these errors may show an attempt at phonetic spelling. Children who make such errors have problems in phonological processes and in visual memory (lexical processes). Not surprisingly, they often have evidence of wider language difficulties.

Helping your child with specific spelling difficulty

The importance of spelling should not be overemphasized; many people become accomplished writers despite poor spelling ability. This is because expressive language skills are separate from spelling skills. Spelling should not be regarded as an end in itself. Although primary school years place great emphasis on learning to spell, inaccuracies in spelling are often ignored in later school years, provided that the writing is comprehensible. Nevertheless, a high school child whose assignments and examination papers are filled with elementary spelling errors will often be at a disadvantage because of the poor impression this makes on the examiner.

Prior to developing a plan for helping your child with his spelling, an assessment should be carried out to determine if a cause for his problem can be found. A spelling programme should cater for the child's particular pattern of difficulties. For example, a child who has phonetic difficulties may need to be trained to break down words into their component parts, a child with auditory discrimination problems may need more training in auditory discrimination, while a child with lexical (visual retention) problems may need practice that emphasizes remembering the appearance of words.

Many children with spelling difficulties, especially if associated with reading difficulties, benefit from a teaching programme that links reading with spelling. The grapheme–phoneme correspondences can then be learned following the same procedures when writing and reading.

Parents play a vital role in helping their child to practise spelling; yet few parents know how best to do this. The common method of the parent asking the child to spell words he has memorized from a list is unsatisfactory for children with a specific spelling difficulty. I shall, therefore, describe another method where the parent has a much more active and positive role in helping the child learn to spell. This method is good for children with poor phonetic or visual retention skills.

First, you should aim to teach your child only a small number of words each day; three is usually sufficient.

Choose a time when you are both feeling relaxed and when you will not be disturbed. The teaching sessions should be carried out with plenty of encouragement in accordance with the suggestions in Chapter 4.

The session should last only about 15 minutes and should preferably take place each day. Short, regular prac-tice sessions are better than long, less frequent sessions.

Before the session, choose the words to be taught from the list provided by the school. Break up each word into parts and write each part on a blank white card. For example, write 'correct' as 'cor' on one card, and 'rect' on another; 'hippopotamus' as 'hip', 'po', 'pot', 'a', and 'mus' on five separate cards. Notice how double letters are always separated.

Sit opposite your child at a well-lit table. Place the cards making up the first word to be taught in the correct sequence in front of the child. Ask him to read the word aloud. Then collect the cards and place them in front of the child one at a time (Figure 7). Ask him to look at the card while you wait four seconds (count silently and slowly 'one-and', 'two-and', 'three-and', 'four-and'). While your child is looking at the card, observe him to make certain that his gaze does not wander. Then ask him

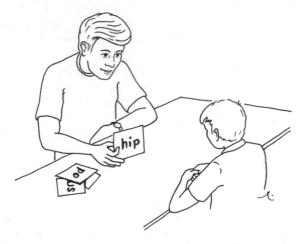

Figure 7. A parent teaching a child to spell (see text for explanation).

to read the card. Move on to the next card and repeat the procedure until all the cards have been looked at and read in turn. Now repeat the process working through the word again, card by card. When this has been completed, remove the cards and give your child a blank sheet of paper. Ask him to write the whole word from memory on the sheet of paper. If he writes the word correctly give him plenty of praise; if he has difficulty spelling the word, dictate it to him slowly, section by section.

Now move on to the next word, teaching each new word in the same manner. Do not rush the procedure, even if your child wants to take short cuts.

At the beginning of the next session, dictate the words your child has already learned and see if he can spell them. If he gets a word correct, praise him. If he cannot spell a word, get out the cards for the word and go through the procedure for teaching a new word again.

You should expect that words will need to be taught a number of times before the child can spell them reliably. If your child cannot spell a word he has already learned, say something like, 'That was a good try, let me get out the cards of this word and you can look at them one by one'. The whole process of 'playing cards' to learn spelling should be treated in a warm, positive manner. End the session with a statement like, 'That was terrific, let's do it again tomorrow'.

In this method of teaching, the parent is helping to break up the words into sections, giving the child time, and encouragement, to memorize each section, and then testing the child in such a way that there is opportunity for success.

Another way of helping a child with his spelling is through the use of computer spelling programs. Educational software can be bought for a home computer, or small computer 'toys' can be purchased that are pre-programmed to teach spelling. An example of the latter is the '*Spelling B Electronic Learning Aid*' manufactured by Texas Instruments.

Software and preprogrammed computers must be carefully selected, so that they are educationally sound. An example of a good program is one that shows a picture and then asks the child to type the correct spelling, giving him a reward if he does. This sort of program will often motivate a child to spend more time practising his spelling because he finds it enjoyable. There is a danger that instead of doing the spelling program, the child will play other computer games, so supervision is needed. Sometimes the other games can be used as a reward for time spent practising spelling.

Spelling dictionaries

Looking up a word in an ordinary dictionary requires knowledge of how the word is spelt. There are special dictionaries that are very useful for children with specific spelling difficulty.[1] In these dictionaries, words are entered under the correct spelling in black, and alternative, incorrect spellings are entered in red. If the child wants to look up knife, for example, he will find it under both 'k' ('knife') and 'n' ('nife'). 'Nife' would be in red and would have the correct spelling next to it.

A more sophisticated solution is the small 'computer dictionary'.[2] This is the size of a hand-held calculator and stores approximately 100 000 words with phonetic corrections. The child can type in 'SYKOLEGY', for example, then press the 'spell' button, and the little screen will show 'PSYCHOLOGY'.

---

[1] Pergamon Dictionary of Perfect Spelling (Arnold–Wheaton) and The Australian Spelling Dictionary (Wileman).
[2] 'WordFinder' Model 224, manufactured by Selectronics.

7 Writing

When David was 12 years old it became apparent that he was having significant difficulty writing. He struggled on, but his writing did not improve and he was regularly having his work returned by teachers because it was illegible. If he tried to write painstakingly slowly he could produce work that was barely legible, but there was not enough time to do this during examinations.

David was very intelligent, an avid reader, an excellent debater, and good at sports. He was well coordinated in every manual task except writing, and was physically healthy. No cause for his difficulty could be found.

At high school and university, he was given permission to type his examination papers and obtained excellent results. He is now a professor of law. He still cannot write legibly, but has had many papers and a number of books published. He uses a combination of dictation and typing instead of writing.

This chapter deals with the mechanics of handwriting, that is, the formation of letters and their arrangement on the page. In contrast with disorders of reading and spelling, such difficulties have received little attention. This is partly because writing is a skill that cannot be easily evaluated by standardized tests, and partly because significant impairment of writing skill seems to be relatively uncommon. Unfortunately, this lack of knowledge means that children with specific writing difficulty are often misunderstood and maligned.

How writing is assessed

Assessment of writing should form part of a comprehensive assessment, as described in Chapter 2.

It is impossible to score a sample of writing in a precise way. In practice, samples of writing are usually evaluated by an experienced tester. Three samples of writing are obtained: a passage of free composition on a particular topic, a piece of dictation, and a copy of some printed material. In the case of the free composition, the child is usually given a limited amount of time, such as five minutes. In the other two tests, he is timed to see how long he takes.

In this way, the tester can see how quickly the child writes, as well as assess the legibility of the samples and study them to determine the nature of the child's difficulties. He or she will also observe the child's posture and method of holding the pen or pencil. In addition to the writing test, the psychologist may do other tests, such as tests of drawing and visual perception.

The doctor will assess the child for the presence of motor (movement) or visual impairment. He or she will establish if the child has evidence of weakness, and whether a tremor or other involuntary movement of the hands is interfering with writing.

Criteria for diagnosis

Without the benefit of standardized tests, the tester will need to make an estimation of whether the difficulty in writing is significant or not. This is similar to the way many conditions are diagnosed in medical practice. For example, conditions such as asthma, epilepsy, and migraine are not diagnosed by standardized testing, but by a characteristic picture and the exclusion of other conditions that may give rise to similar findings.

In practice, the diagnosis of a significant impairment in writing skill is usually not difficult. Figures 8–10 show three samples of writing. Figure 8 shows the neat writing of a normal 10-year-old. Figure 9 shows the writing of another 10-year-old. This is less uniform, but clearly does not represent a significant difficulty; it lies well within the average range. By contrast, the writing in Figure 10, also by a 10-year-old, is unquestionably abnormal. Such illegible writing, despite great effort, is clearly abnormal at this age.

When specific writing difficulty is detected

Specific writing difficulty is often present in children with specific reading difficulty. In these children, writing

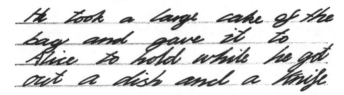

Figure 8. The handwriting of a normal 10-year-old.

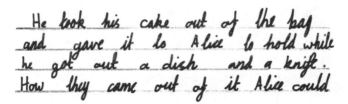

Figure 9. The handwriting of a normal 10-year-old.

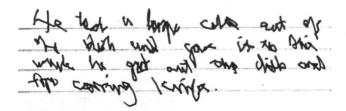

Figure 10. Specific writing difficulty (10-year-old).

difficulty may first be detected when the reading difficulty is assessed.

In some children, such as David described above, specific writing difficulty is an isolated problem. When specific writing difficulty occurs on its own, it may not be detected until late primary or even high school. This often takes parents by surprise as they wonder why the difficulty was not noticed earlier. The late diagnosis seems to be related to the nature of the demands for writing made on children at school. Unlike reading, where the child performs in front of the teacher, written work is often not seen by the teacher until it is finished. Children with specific writing difficulty may be able to produce legible writing if they are allowed very long periods of time. (This is analogous to a right-hander writing laboriously with his left hand.) Figure 11 shows the writing of the same boy as in Figure 10. The sample of writing in Figure 11 was produced over a period of thirty-five minutes, while the writing in Figure 10 was produced in five minutes. The writing shown in Figure 11 required a tremendous amount of sustained effort but is now legible. Children with specific writing difficulty can often produce acceptable work by spending long periods of time writing it out at home. They often become very skilled at 'forgetting' to hand in work, making excuses for delays, and even getting others to do their writing for them. By high school, though, speed of writing becomes more important than neatness, and the child's difficulty is

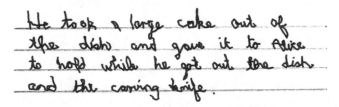

Figure 11. The writing of the child in Figure 10, when allowed unlimited time.

discovered. It is often initially mistaken for laziness. This is likely to occur because writing for these children is very fatiguing and they often become tired after a short period. They become increasingly discouraged and may eventually refuse to write.

Defects in specific writing difficulty

The exact nature of the writing difficulty varies from child to child. The commonest problems are motor planning difficulties and visual perception deficit.

Motor planning difficulties

In this problem the child can produce any of the actions involved in forming a letter in isolation, but the part of the brain responsible for ensuring that these actions are carried out in an uninterrupted sequence does not work properly. This is a well-recognized problem, known as dyspraxia; it is also seen in adults who have sustained damage to certain parts of the brain. It may be associated with generalized clumsiness and with speech problems (verbal dyspraxia).

Visual perception deficit

Whereas motor planning difficulties affect the way that letters are produced, visual perception deficit affects the way in which they are perceived. Children with this deficit have an impairment in the way in that they perceive the shape and configuration of letters. This is not due to a disorder of the eyes, but to a problem with the way the brain interprets the messages transmitted from the eyes.

Such children will be shown to have difficulties on tests of visual perception. They often go about making letters in an extremely complicated and uncomfortable way. They may superimpose letters, write them the wrong way round, or leave large gaps between letters.

Pencil grip disorders

Low muscular tone in the small muscles of the hands is sometimes suggested as the reason for specific writing difficulty. Muscular tone is ascertained by the degree of resistance felt when a tester moves relaxed muscles. Low tone, therefore, implies a certain 'floppiness' of muscles.

While the tone in the hand muscles of some children with writing difficulty is low, it is unlikely that this is the whole explanation for their difficulties. In such cases, an additional problem, such as dyspraxia or visual perception deficit, is usually present. It is only in very rare cases that extremely low tone combined with very lax joint ligaments of the hand makes the hand so unstable that it is difficult to control the pencil.

Visual memory deficit

This is a defect that occurs in the rare child who copies well, but is unable to write from dictation. The defect is in the ability to remember the shape of the letters.

Spatial planning deficit

This would explain those children who have particular difficulty arranging their writing on the page.

Diminished rate of processing

This may occur in children whose writing is very slow. The process of writing is normal, but so slowed down that if the child attempts to go at normal speed, the writing becomes disorganized.

Which form of writing should be taught?

The most fluent form of writing is cursive writing (Figure 12, line 3), where the letters are joined and the pen is only lifted off the paper between words. However, a child

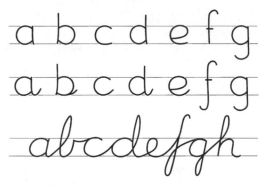

Figure 12. Three forms of writing: manuscript (first line), precursive (middle line), and cursive (bottom line).

who is beginning to write will usually have great difficulty learning this form of writing straight away. It is for this reason that either manuscript writing (Figure 12, line 1) or precursive writing (Figure 12, line 2) is taught first.

Children with severe writing difficulty are best taught manuscript writing as it is the simplest form of writing. Some of these children will not progress beyond this stage. This need not be a disadvantage as manuscript writing can be legible, is legally acceptable, and can become quite rapid.

Children whose writing difficulty is not so severe are often taught precursive writing rather than manuscript writing. In precursive writing many of the letters end in curved strokes (ligatures). This makes it easier for children to progress to cursive writing later. Another advantage of this form of writing, compared with manuscript writing, is that the ligatures make it easier for the child to distinguish between similar letters (such as 'b' and 'd'). This is helpful for children who confuse such letters.

It should be noted that in precursive writing, ligatures are added to the ends of letters, but not the beginnings. This is because the way a ligature joins the beginning of a letter is determined by the letter that precedes it (Figure 13). The

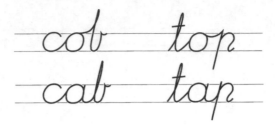

Figure 13. When 'b' or 'p' are preceded by an 'o', the ligature joins them close to the upper line. When they are preceded by an 'a', the ligature joins them close to the baseline.

child should be taught that the ligature belongs to the letter that precedes it.

After a few years, the transition from precursive to cursive writing occurs naturally in many children. Others need to be taught how to join letters, slope their writing slightly to the right, and modify some of the letters, such as 'b', 'p', and 'f', to their cursive forms.

Helping your child with specific writing difficulty

Children with specific writing difficulty often suffer in silence. The acknowledgement that they have a problem that is not their fault is often of great comfort to them.

Occupational therapists provide advice and help with handwriting. Some have particular experience in this field and have developed special expertise in helping children with poor handwriting. Some teachers will have special skills in helping children with handwriting difficulties.

Analysis of the way the child sits and holds the pen is important, but it should be borne in mind that this is usually not a major part of the problem. There is no set of hard and fast rules about writing that applies to all children. Allowances should be made for individual differences. The younger the child, the easier it is to change the child's posture and pencil grip. In an older child, it may be necessary to accept awkward postures that are very difficult to change and to concentrate on how the letters are formed.

Figures 14–16 show the ideal writing positions for right- and left-handers. Note that the child should be encouraged to hold the paper or book with his non-writing hand; he should not use it to support his head. A foot rest is helpful if the child's feet cannot reach the floor. Non-slip mats under the writing surface may also be needed. Good lighting is essential.

Figure 17 shows the ideal 'dynamic tripod' pencil grip. Many children have variations on this grip that they use with success, but the 'dagger' grip (Figure 18) and the 'hook' posture of the left-hander (Figure 19) should be discouraged. Usually, the best first writing implement is an HB pencil. A plastic pencil grip, such as the one shown in Figure 20, may be helpful.

In the early stages of learning to write, letters are often formed very large and may fill the page. Initially, blank sheets of paper may be used. Later, the child will learn to

Figure 14. The ideal sitting position for writing. The back is straight, the forearms rest comfortably on the writing surface, and the feet are flat on the floor with the knees comfortably flexed.

Figure 15. The ideal position for cursive writing (right-hander). For manuscript writing, the paper does not need to be placed at a slant.

Figure 16. The ideal position for cursive writing (left-hander). For manuscript writing, the paper does not need to be placed at a slant.

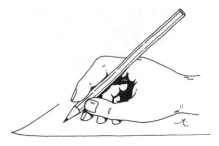

Figure 17. 'Dynamic tripod' grip.

Figure 18. 'Dagger' grip.

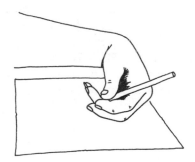

Figure 19. 'Hook' position (left-hander).

reduce the size of the letters and lined paper can then be introduced. Sometimes, squared paper or paper with special lines is needed.

It is best if the occupational therapist, or teacher, breaks up the task of writing the letters into steps, so that

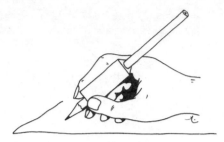

Figure 20. A plastic pencil grip.

the child can practice each step in isolation. This teaching may be multisensory, with the child tracing the shape of the letter with his fingers in sand, walking in the formation of the letter, and having the letter traced on his skin. This may be helpful, but the emphasis should still be on writing on paper.

Letters with similar starting points and shapes should be taught in groups (Figure 21). When children first learn to form letters, this is usually done by tracing them. When tracing is accomplished, they can learn to copy them, and, finally, to write them from dictation. In the early stage of copying, the child may benefit from marks on the paper showing him where to start each letter.

To make writing practice more interesting, the therapist may devise games and attractive materials for writing practice. As the child becomes neater with his writing, he

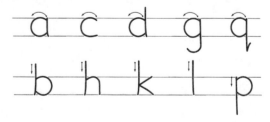

Figure 21. Letters should be taught in groups with similar starting points and shapes. The top line shows some of the 'c' group, and the bottom line shows some of the 'l' group.

may enjoy writing a letter to a friend, or copying the words of favourite songs, stories, or jokes. There should be plenty of praise for effort.

For children who cannot fulfil their need to express themselves because of writing difficulty, a typewriter or portable computer may be needed. In such a situation the advantages of easier expression will need to be weighed up against the possibility that the child will abandon further attempts to improve his writing.

Electronic typewriters are now quiet and portable, and schools are more accepting of their use in the classroom. It may be possible to obtain funding for such equipment from a government department or a local service organization.

For many children with writing difficulty, a typewriter or computer is an invaluable solution to their problem. Not only can they often be taught to type well, but as they learn to type, they may develop a better awareness of the sequence of letters in words.

8
Arithmetic

Specific difficulties have been described in a number of areas of mathematics, but difficulty in arithmetic has received the most attention. This may be because all children are required to do arithmetical calculations in the early years of school, but can choose alternative subjects later, and it probably also reflects the fact that arithmetical calculations play an important part in everyday life. Another reason may be that arithmetical difficulty following brain damage in adulthood (dyscalculia) is a well-recognized and well-studied entity.

This chapter will focus on specific arithmetic difficulty in children, that is, unexplained, significant delay in arithmetic ability. Although specific arithmetic difficulty was once considered rare, there is now evidence that it is not as uncommon as was previously thought.

How arithmetic skills are tested

The psychologist may obtain sufficient information about the child's arithmetical ability from the Arithmetic section (sub-test) of the Wechsler Intelligence Scale for Children (WISC). This is a commonly used intelligence test that can be used for children from 6 years to 16 years 11 months. This test does not require the child to write down the answers. The problems are timed and they relate to various arithmetical skills. Addition, subtraction, multiplication, and division can all be tested. Some problems also require memorized number facts and subtle operations, such as seeing relevant relationships at a glance. The emphasis of the test is not on mathematical knowledge as such, but on mental computations and concentration.

The WISC will also give the psychologist information about other abilities, which may shed light on the child's difficulties. In the Digit Span sub-test, the child's ability to remember numbers for a short period is tested. In the Comprehension sub-test, verbal reasoning is involved. If, for example, a child has high comprehension but low arithmetic scores, this may suggest that reasoning ability is adequate in social situations, but not in situations involving numbers.

If the psychologist wants further information on arithmetic ability, there are a number of tests that specifically test mathematical skills and allow these to be compared with those of other children of the same age.

Types of difficulty

Some skills involved in solving arithmetical problems are used only for such functions, while other overlap with other areas of learning. Children with problems in the latter group may therefore have difficulties in other areas as well.

- Arithmetic problems require language comprehension skills (the ability to understand the words used to explain the problem), and so specific arithmetic difficulty may be associated with *language disorders*.

- Reading ability is required to understand a written arithmetical problem, so there is an association with *reading difficulty*.

- *Writing difficulty* may interfere with the ability to write down numbers and symbols.

- Problems with revisualization (remembering) of numbers may be associated with difficulties revisualizing words, so specific arithmetic difficulty may be associated with *spelling difficulty*.

In some children, specific arithmetic difficulty may be an isolated problem owing to difficulties with skills largely confined to arithmetic. The difficulties that such children have are many and varied. Some of the deficits involve the areas detailed below.

Mathematical comprehension

This is the ability to understand what a number represents. A child with difficulties in this area would, for example, be able to write the number 'seven', but would not realize that it comes before eight.

Operational functions

This is the ability to add, subtract, multiply, or divide. A child with a difficulty in this area would, for example, continue to rely on his fingers for simple calculations. To overcome their problem, such children may devise their own methods for carrying out calculations.

Selection process

This is the ability to select the appropriate arithmetical operation to solve a problem. Children with difficulty in this skill can carry out an operation, such as addition or division, when it is specified, but cannot decide which operation to carry out when given a word problem where the appropriate operation is not specified.

Sequential memory

This is the ability to remember the order of operations required to solve a problem.

Sequential organization

This is the ability to establish numerical order. Children with difficulty in this skill may have problems learning the multiplication tables. This may be related to other difficulties in sequential organization (see Chapter 10).

Verbal mathematics expression

This is the ability to express mathematical terms and concepts in words.

Abstract symbolization

This is the ability to understand the representation of numbers by symbols. Children with difficulty in this area will have particular problems in algebra.

Auditory–visual associations

This is the ability to identify a number with a written symbol. Children with difficulty in this skill may count well, but be unable to read numbers.

Clustering

This is the ability to discern or identify groups of objects (sets). Children with difficulty in this skill have to count objects individually.

Concrete mathematical manipulation

This is the ability to judge the size and number of actual objects, such as cubes and rods. Children with difficulty in this skill have problems when required to do hands-on manipulations involving these objects. This is often un-expected, because most people find concrete manipulations easier than abstract calculations.

Conservation of quantity

This is the ability to understand that quantity does not change with shape. For example, if liquid is poured from a short, wide container into a narrow, high one, the volume of liquid remains the same. Most children first begin to understand this during the early school years. Some older children can be shown not to have grasped this concept.

Establishment of one-to-one correspondence

The ability to deal with constant mathematical proportions. Children with difficulty in this skill may, for example, not be able to allocate three cubes to three children.

Graphic representation of numbers

This is the ability to remember and write down numbers.

Interpreting process signs

This is the ability to read and understand arithmetical symbols such as '+', and '–'. Children with difficulty in this area may be extremely slow in working out what such a sign means when they see it written down.

Helping your child with specific arithmetic difficulty

As we can see, arithmetic involves many different skills, and difficulties can be due to deficits in any one of these. It is, therefore, essential that a careful analysis of the exact nature of the child's problem is undertaken. For example, if a child is having difficulty with multiplication, it could be a result of difficulties with interpreting process signs, auditory–visual associations, abstract symbolization, sequential organization, mathematical comprehension, operational functions, selection process, or long-term memory. An attempt should be made to establish which of these is the cause, so that appropriate help can be given.

With the great variety of methods for teaching arithmetic now used in schools, it is essential that you discuss your child's difficulties with his teacher. If you try to teach him a different method of solving problems to that taught by the teacher, it could confuse him.

Parents often feel that their own mathematical skills are too rudimentary to allow them to teach their child. In this situation you may be able to arrange for your child to have extra lessons in mathematics after school. The teacher should have a good grasp of mathematics and be able to anticipate the difficulties the child may have, in order to devise methods of solving problems that are as easy as possible for the child to learn. Individual tuition on a one-to-one basis can pay great dividends.

You can always help your child with arithmetical concepts and arithmetical practice in everyday situations. Discuss things that involve numbers with him, and encourage him to take part in activities that involve counting, such as laying the table (he needs to count how many knives to take out of the drawer, and so on), making small purchases on his own, playing games with a dice (such as 'Ludo' and 'Snakes and ladders'), and cooking (measuring ingredients).

Children with specific arithmetic difficulty often experience intense anxiety whenever they are presented with an arithmetic problem that they have to solve. It is interesting that many articles have been written on 'arithmetic anxiety', but hardly any on anxiety associated with reading or spelling. The reason that arithmetic seems more likely to engender fear and distress in children is unknown. It is therefore important that arithmetic is taught in an encouraging and positive manner. Try to make it as much fun as possible for you and the child.

When teaching a child with specific arithmetic difficulty, it is often necessary to return to basics and teach the child skills such as counting, addition, and subtraction all over again. Some teachers show great ingenuity in finding enjoyable ways of teaching children these skills. This is important so that the child's self-esteem is enhanced. It is also important because a large component of mathematical skill development involves repeated practice, something that children are far more likely to do if they enjoy it.

If you need to take responsibility for teaching arithmetic to your child you may feel daunted when you look at his arithmetic text books. Remember that the basic arithmetic taught to children is not very complex, and remains fundamentally the same no matter what syllabus is followed. The child should go through the following stages, consolidating each stage before going to the next.

Stage 1: numbers, counting, sorting, matching, and arranging in order

Children should first learn to count and to recognize numbers. They should then sort objects into groups, before learning to match objects by size, colour, and shape. They should then learn how to arrange numbers in order.

Stage 2: addition, subtraction, multiplication, and division

Adding is a form of counting (2 + 2 is another way of saying, start with two and then count a further two). Children may need to use concrete objects (such as blocks or fingers) at first.

Subtraction is counting backwards (5 − 2 is another way of saying, start with five and then count two backwards). Children are often taught adding and subtracting using a number line (Figure 22).

Children are usually encouraged to learn the link between addition and multiplication before memorizing

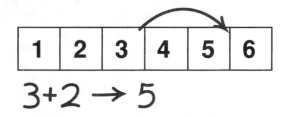

Figure 22. A number line.

multiplication tables (2×3 is another way of adding two sets of three).

Division is often introduced as sharing ($8 \div 2$ is eight apples shared between two children).

Stage 3: measurement, shape, time, and money

Measurement is now taught by 'hands-on' experience. Objects are measured for length, and later for volume and weight.

Concepts such as volume, capacity, shapes, angles, time, and money are all introduced by giving children as much practical experience as possible.

Calculators and computers

A child who has difficulty with arithmetic calculations may be greatly helped by a calculator. These can now be so small and light that they are unobtrusive. The decision to introduce a calculator should be made in consultation with the teacher. A child who is being kept back by difficulties with arithmetical operations may benefit from a calculator. However, if the calculator is introduced prematurely, the child may lose the opportunity to become better at performing calculations quickly in his head.

There are a number of programmes for teaching or practising arithmetic on a computer, as well as preprogrammed computer toys for practising arithmetic. Some of these are small and can also be used as portable calculators (for example, 'Dataman' which is manufactured by Texas Instruments). Many are cleverly designed and very entertaining.

When using a computer, there is always the danger that, instead of doing the arithmetic programme, the child will play other computer games, so supervision is needed. Sometimes the other games can be used as a reward for time spent practising arithmetic.

Language

Vanessa was first seen at the clinic one year ago, at the age of eight years. Her teacher had reported that she seemed 'slower' than the other children in the class. She observed that Vanessa often did not understand what was going on in the class, and was easily upset by changes in routine. She also had difficulties expressing her ideas and relating her experiences. Her reading, spelling, and writing were all behind those of the rest of the class.

A psychologist's assessment showed Vanessa's non-verbal intelligence to be in the average range, but with difficulties in comprehension. Her reading, spelling, and writing all showed more than two years' delay. A doctor could find no abnormalities to account for her problem. Her hearing was tested and found to be normal.

Vanessa was referred to a speech therapist. She found that Vanessa's comprehension was at a level more than two years below her age and that she had many difficulties in her understanding of language. For example, although she understood common prepositions such as 'in', 'on', and 'under', she misinterpreted others such as 'beside', 'behind', 'through', and 'around'. She also confused past and present tenses.

The speech therapist spoke to the parents and the teacher about ways of helping Vanessa. She also started seeing her regularly, once a week, for speech therapy sessions. Now, after 10 months of such help, Vanessa has shown great improvement in her language comprehension and her academic skills.

Language plays a central role in specific learning difficulties. Reading requires the ability to decode written language and spelling and writing require the ability to encode spoken language. Arithmetic requires language skills to understand the words used to state problems involving numbers.

This chapter deals with the disorders of speech and language that often accompany specific learning difficulties. These may involve the understanding of language (which is referred to as receptive language) and the use of language (which is referred to as expressive language). There may also be involvement of speech (which relates to the clarity and fluency of the spoken word).

How language is assessed

A child with suspected language difficulties should be assessed by a speech therapist (sometimes called a speech pathologist). Such an assessment involves both informal observation and standardized tests to evaluate speech, expressive language, and receptive language. In addition to establishing the child's level of development in these areas, the speech therapist will determine the specific nature of his difficulties.

It is essential that every child with speech or language delay also has a thorough test of his hearing, as hearing impairment is a possible cause of such delays.

Normal language development during the school years

Most parents are aware how much language is learned during the early years of childhood, yet many do not appreciate how much language development occurs during the school years. This development is critical to the child's ability to cope with both the academic and the social aspects of schooling.

During the school years, children rapidly expand their vocabulary. They also develop a far more complex understanding of the content, form, and use of language.

When they enter school, they already have competent language skills, but these are more automatic than analytical. By the age of seven or eight, most children make a shift from using concrete reasoning to more conceptual reasoning (syntagmatic/paradigmatic shift). For example, when asked to tell how a watch and a clock are alike, the young child may say that they both tick, or that they are both round—he is focusing on what he can hear and see. The older child, on the other hand, may answer that they both tell the time, thus showing that he can now form more abstract concepts.

As the child develops, he understands more complex syntax. For example, he can understand that 'Before you give him the money, ask how much it costs' means the same as 'First ask him how much it costs, then give him the money'.

Another change is in the child's ability to understand literary usage, which requires knowledge of language styles not needed in everyday conversation. For example, in a conversation one might say 'When it got dark he went home.' In literate language this may be written, 'As night began to fall, he went home.' As children develop they are able to understand and use advanced literate language. This is important for their ability to succeed academically.

A particularly important aspect of the changes that occur during the school years is in the development of what are known as metalinguistic skills. These refer to the ability to analyse and reflect on language itself. This plays an important part in the child's ability to understand metaphors, idioms, riddles, puns, jokes, and many other linguistic devices and nuances. Understanding of these is important for social as well as academic competence.

Components of language

When a child responds to a question, a number of things happen. First, he must attend to what is being asked (attention). He must then be able to hear each sound (hearing), and to discriminate between different sounds (auditory discrimination). If a word is known, the brain will draw upon a store of remembered words. This process requires the ability to store and retrieve words (language memory) and their meanings (semantics).

Understanding language is not just a matter of decoding individual words. The way in which words are arranged in sentences provides major clues to their meaning, so to understand the meaning of sentences the brain must have circuits that analyse grammatical (syntactic) structure. Unfamiliar words need to be broken down into their component parts (segmentation) before they may be understood or repeated.

However, understanding communication is more than just understanding words and sentences. When we listen to speech we may comprehend without attending to every word sound. We infer meaning from clues, from how things are put, and from the intonation of the speaker's voice. This ability is an important part of understanding (metalinguistic awareness).

Once the spoken word has been understood, the complex process of generating expressive language must be initiated. After the response has been planned, words must be retrieved from the semantic store and arranged with the aid of syntactic skills. Word sounds will need to be combined (blended) to make words and sentences.

These are just some of the steps involved in language. Children may have difficulty with any one of these steps, or with a number of steps. This makes precise analysis of a child's difficulties very complicated: any attempt to classify language difficulties has to be a simplification.

Types of language difficulty

Although there are many types of difficulty in speech and language, there are three important types that are associated with specific learning difficulties. These are expressive language difficulty, receptive language (comprehension) difficulty, and verbal dyspraxia.

Expressive language difficulty

This is the commonest language difficulty. It may be a result of a variety of blocks in the stages of language production.

Typically, the child's speech sounds immature for his age, with difficulties naming things. He may omit words from sentences and mix the order of words. His written language will also show these features (Figure 23).

Children with expressive language difficulties are often frustrated by their difficulties in expressing themselves, and may be shy and withdrawn. Some become short tempered because of their frustration. Expressive language difficulties are often associated with reading difficulties.

It is essential that any child with suspected expressive language delay has an assessment by a speech therapist. The therapist will test the child's receptive and expressive language. He or she may also want a sample of the child's spontaneous language at home. Parents may, therefore, be asked to make a tape recording of their child's speech in an everyday situation.

Once the speech therapist has analysed the child's difficulties and developed a picture of his language, he or she can plan a programme to help the child. Most speech therapists will want to see the child for regular therapy sessions. These usually take place once a week or once a fortnight.

The therapist will tailor the programme to the child's needs. This usually involves showing the child objects

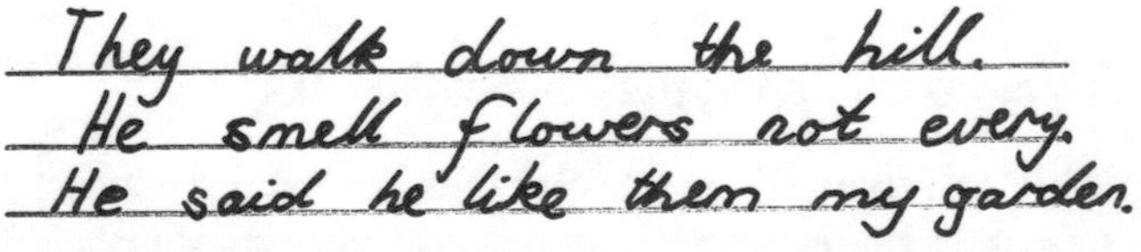

> They walk down the hill.
> He smell flowers not every.
> He said he like them my garden.

Figure 23. Expressive language disorder (nine-year-old boy).

and pictures, which he names or talks about. Games and exercises involving certain words and grammatical structures are worked on, and there is training in sentence construction. The nature of the help will depend on the child's specific difficulties.

How parents can help

The speech therapist will tell you what to do at home. Often he or she will give you a book, or sheets of paper, with games and activities to play. These should be carried out with a sense of fun and plenty of praise for effort. You will also be told how to encourage the child to carry over what he is learning into everyday conversation. Try to use those particular language structures that your child is learning as much as possible in your own speech to serve as an example (model) for him.

Receptive language (comprehension) difficulty

Difficulties in comprehension can be easily missed in the school-aged child. Parents may not realize how much such a child does not understand, because he copes by using non-verbal clues. At home, the child may use the context to infer what is required of him. Many parents are not aware how much they use facial expression and hand gestures to convey meaning to their child. At school the child may take his lead from the other children.

In a child with difficulties, such as those described in Vanessa at the beginning of this chapter, subtle difficulties in understanding can easily be interpreted as laziness or disobedience. They can also be interpreted as being due to a lack of intelligence. But comprehension is only one aspect of intelligence and children can have specific delays in language comprehension and have normal intelligence.

The typical pattern seen in children of school age with receptive language delay is that they miss or misinterpret some of what is said to them. Their difficulties may be confined to certain words, or classes of words, or certain concepts or grammatical structures.

Children with receptive language delay may be socially competent despite their difficulties. However, some are very shy and say little in the company of other children. Some appear slightly aloof and self-absorbed. These characteristics are related to their language difficulty, and usually disappear once this resolves.

Children with suspected receptive language delay should always have an assessment by a speech therapist. In addition, their hearing should be tested. They should also be examined by a doctor, as there are a number of rare medical conditions that cause receptive language delay.

The speech therapist will institute a programme to teach the child better language comprehension. He or she will find ways of teaching the meaning of words and grammatical structures.

How parents can help

Parents should reinforce the work carried out by the speech therapist. He or she will give you instructions on what to do at home. Parents have the opportunity to extend their child's understanding of language in many different situations and environments.

When speaking to your child, always speak slowly and clearly, pausing after each phrase. Make certain he has understood; repeat what you have said if necessary. Praise appropriate responses. It may be necessary to use gestures if your child cannot understand; your speech therapist will advise you on whether this is appropriate.

Request that your child sits near the front of the class. Explain the nature of the problem to the teacher. It is best if the speech therapist also explains this to the teacher so that he or she gains an understanding of the child's difficulties. This is important so that the child is not considered naughty when he does not understand instructions, and it also allows the teacher to incorporate language taught by the speech therapist in the child's curriculum. It is also important that you encourage your child to tell the teacher when he does not understand something.

Verbal dyspraxia

Verbal dyspraxia is a disorder of speech, rather than of language. In this condition, there is a difficulty in carrying out the series of movements required to speak clearly. There is nothing wrong with the chest, vocal cords, throat, or mouth themselves; it is the control of these by the brain that is the problem.

Speaking is the most virtuosic movement children need to carry out. The technical mastery involved in coordinating the movements of the chest, diaphragm, vocal cords, tongue, palate, throat, and lips in order to speak is comparable to that of a violinist playing a piece of music. It has been estimated that the movements for speech require the simultaneous or closely sequenced coordination of over a hundred pairs of different breathing and speaking muscles.

A child with dyspraxia can often make the individual sounds in isolation, but has difficulty when he wants to coordinate these to speak clearly.

Dyspraxia of other purposeful movements (motor dyspraxia) is one of the causes of clumsiness, as I shall describe in Chapter 11. Verbal dyspraxia is, therefore, sometimes associated with general clumsiness. Children with verbal dyspraxia may have a tendency to dribble saliva because of poor swallowing coordination. This usually improves with age.

The child with dyspraxia usually has good language but indistinct speech. Words may be difficult to understand, as sounds are omitted or distorted by the 'clumsy mouth'. Language problems may coexist with dyspraxia, making the picture more complicated.

If the speech therapist finds that a child has verbal dyspraxia, he or she will commence regular therapy sessions to improve the clarity of the child's speech. This usually involves working on individual sounds at first and then words and phrases.

Often, children with verbal dyspraxia do not realize how indistinct their speech is. It is sometimes necessary to give them feedback about their speech. Recordings of the child's voice may be helpful. Sometimes children are helped by seeing their mouth movements in a mirror.

How parents can help

Parents play an important part in providing an opportunity for their child to continue exercises at home. The speech therapist will advise you how to go about this. Activities should be enjoyable for the child and there should be praise for effort. Parents can help their child to carry over his improved speech into everyday communication. This is difficult for the child at first, and the speech therapist will guide you when and how to remind him to speak slowly and clearly.

10 Attention deficit disorder and sequential organization difficulties

This chapter deals with two separate areas of learning: attention and sequential organization. Difficulties in either area can occur in isolation, or in combination with other forms of specific learning difficulty.

Attention deficit disorder

The ability to ignore distractions and to focus on one activity at a time is a skill that children usually develop gradually as they grow. It is quite normal for toddlers and pre-school-aged children to be easily distractable, but the ability to channel attention selectively usually increases progressively once children start school.

Some children experience significant difficulties in learning to attend. As a result, they are easily distractable and do not persist for long with tasks. If this is a significant problem, it is referred to as 'attention dificit disorder'.

Such children may also be overactive and impulsive, although this is not always the case. It is this overactivity that has given rise to the term hyperactivity ('hyper' is Greek for 'over').

All children with attention deficit disorder experience difficulty with concentration. There are two forms of the condition: one where overactivity and impulsivity are present and the other where these coexisting problems are absent.

The two forms of attention deficit disorder may be clarified by describing two children, each with one of the forms of the disorder.

A child with attention deficit disorder with overactivity and impulsivity

George is his mother's third child. She describes him as completely different from the other two. As a baby he slept very little and cried constantly. As a toddler he was always on the go, 'as if driven by a motor'. Now, aged nine years, his teacher describes him as 'disorganized, disruptive, and fidgety'. His mother reports that he hardly ever sits still at home. He will not sit through a favourite TV programme or a meal. He is still so disorganized that if she did not help him to dress in the morning, he would not be in time for school.

He is also very impulsive. He does not seem to think before he acts. He takes terrible risks and often says the first thing that comes in to his head. The worst thing is that he does not seem to learn from his mistakes.

The school psychologist has tested George. The test was carried out with great difficulty because of George's distractability and tendency to answer questions without thinking. The psychologist found his intelligence to be in the normal range, but his reading, spelling, and arithmetic were all significantly below the average range.

George was then examined by a developmental paediatrician who made a diagnosis of attention deficit disorder. Treatment with appropriate medication and remedial assistance resulted in a dramatic improvement in George's behaviour and learning.

A child with attention deficit disorder without overactivity

Caroline was a bright child who experienced great difficulty learning to read. She was tested by the psychologist attached to her school and a diagnosis of 'dyslexia' was made. Remedial help was commenced early in her school career but Caroline made slow progress. At the age of 11 it was clear she had worked hard but was becoming increasingly discouraged by her difficulties. She was often in tears and started refusing to attend remedial classes. Her parents were very concerned about her as time was running out before she entered high school.

They took her to a developmental paediatrician. He arranged for the educational psychologist in his practice to do further detailed testing of Caroline's difficulties. This, in conjuction with the paediatrician's own findings, led to a diagnosis of dyslexia complicated by attention deficit disorder. Caroline's parents were surprised about the diagnosis of attention deficit disorder as they believed that children with this disorder were overactive while Caroline was a quiet, responsible girl. The developmental paediatrician explained that there are two types of attention deficit disorder: one associated with overactivity and one where this is not present. Caroline had the latter form and this was interfering with her need to concentrate in order to overcome her dyslexia.

Treatment was commenced with medication given on school days only. Remedial help continued as before. Within a matter of days there was a remarkable change in Caroline's attitude to her work. Her mood improved and she became enthusiastic about her ability to concentrate and learn. Six months later her reading had caught up to her age level.

Both George and Caroline have attention deficit disorder and yet their behaviour is very different. Children such as George are often diagnosed at a young age, children like Caroline often do not receive appropriate treatment until high school.

A diagnosis of attention deficit disorder should only be made after information about the child has been carefully collected, and the child has been observed by an experienced development paediatrician working in collaboration with an educational psychologist. It is essential that the opinion of the child's teacher is obtained to determine the nature of the child's behaviour at school. All other possible causes, such as emotional and environmental stresses, should be searched for and excluded before a diagnosis of attention deficit disorder is made.

When diagnosed in this way, attention deficit disorder is approximately five times more common in males. Often there is a history of similar difficulties in other family relatives. It may occur on its own, but often accompanies other forms of specific learning difficulty.

The major feature of such children is their poor persistence with tasks. They often fail to finish things they start. They are easily distracted, do not seem to listen, and have difficulty concentrating on school work and other tasks requiring sustained attention.

What parents can do

Children with attention deficit disorder who are impulsive can be very trying to live with. It is important to realize that your child's behaviour is not your fault or the fault of your child, who may have great difficulty fulfilling expectations.

It is important to set appropriate goals for your child. For example, you may initially expect him to remain at the table for only five minutes, and then gradually increase your expectations. Be generous with your praise when goals are achieved.

If he is overactive give him an opportunity to burn off extra energy with active play. A trampoline is good in this respect. Swimming is also a good way to get rid of pent-up energy. Allow him to go out even if it's raining. Rain will not harm him, but staying indoors for protracted periods can be very trying for all concerned.

If possible, avoid restrictive, confusing, and overstimulating places if your child seems to be adversely affected by these.

When you give your child an instruction, make sure that you have his attention. It may be necessary to touch him gently and make certain that he is looking at you. When speaking to him talk slowly, and pause after each phrase.

Behaviour management advice

Parents of children who are impulsive often benefit from professional advice about ways of helping their child. The doctor who makes the diagnosis will either provide you with this advice, or be able to refer you to someone who will. A professional will help you to monitor behaviour and advise on appropriate techniques for encouraging good behaviour and discouraging unwanted behaviour. He or she will be able to help you identify things that tend to provoke difficult behaviour and also those things that seem to work best at avoiding it.

Diets

The diet promoted by Dr Ben Feingold has received much publicity from the media and parent groups. It involves the exclusion of foods containing certain artificial colouring agents, as well as some naturally occurring substances present in fruits and other foods.

Many controlled trials have been performed and there is evidence that the diet may cause some reduction in overactivity, impulsivity, task impersistence, and distractability in a small proportion of children.

The diet is difficult to keep to in its strict form, but is nutritionally sound provided that care is taken to ensure there is an adequate intake of vitamin C. Many parents report that the diet does help, although fewer feel that it cures the problem. If you feel that your child improves on the diet, there's no reason why you should not keep him on it.

Medicines

In 1937 there was a report of a stimulant drug used in children with hyperactivity that, paradoxically, slowed down some children. Since that time, stimulant drugs have been used for some children with the diagnosis of attention deficit disorder (both with and without hyperactivity). There is now no doubt that about 80 per cent of children do show some response to these drugs. The medicines result in better attention and less disruptive behaviour. Not surprisingly, children on medication are better able to learn and there is often a dramatic improvement in school attainment.

The stimulant medications are short-acting and can be used to cover certain situations where children need to attend closely. Children often take the medication on school days only. Behaviour modification techniques and remedial help should continue while the medication is given.

Not all children with attention deficit disorder respond to the medication. One way to assess whether the medicine is working in a particular child is to arrange for the teacher to monitor the child's performance. He or she must do this without knowing when the child is on the medicine and when he is not. Over a period of four weeks, the medicine is given according to a schedule known only to the doctor and the parents. During this time the teacher keeps a daily record of the child's behaviour. The teacher can use a standard rating scale such as the one that appears in my book, *All About ADD*, (Oxford University Press, 1995). At the end of the period, the parents and teacher compare the teacher's ratings with the pattern of administration of the medicine. The child's behaviour should have shown significant improvement on treatment days if the medicine is to be used. With adequate explanation by the doctors, teachers are usually prepared to take part in this sort of trial.

Some developmental paediatricians test the response to a medication by means of a 'before and after' computer test. This is particularly useful in children without behavioural problems where a teacher's observation may not be helpful. This form of testing involves comparing the child's performance on standardized tests of concentration and memory before and after taking the medicine. This is usually carried out in the paediatrician's rooms.

First, a standardized test is administered to the child. He then takes a dose of the medicine to be evaluated and is required to wait for an hour until the medicine has been absorbed. A second test is then administered which is different from, but of equal difficulty to, the first.

There are many factors that can affect a child's performance over a short period of time, and the results of a first stage trial should be interpreted with care.

If the child's performance on the second test is worse than on the first, this is known as an adverse response. If this occurs, a first stage trial with another medicine, or with a different dose of the same medicine, is usually necessary.

If there is a statistically significant improvement after the medicine, this is known as a positive response. The child may then embark on treatment with that medicine.

Treatment should be under the control of a developmental paediatrician. The need for medication should be kept under regular review and it should be stopped as soon as it is no longer required.

Sequential organization difficulties

Another important area of learning is in 'sequential organization': the ability to get things into the right order. Difficulties in this area are common in children with many forms of specific learning difficulty, and may play a part in causing impairments in some areas such as reading and spelling.

A child with significant difficulty in sequential organization will experience problems with tasks such as following directions, counting, telling time, using a calendar, and getting to know the day's schedule. Such a child will often have difficulty getting dressed quickly, having the correct books ready for a class, getting to the right classroom, and following complex instructions. It may also result in spelling errors such as 'hegde' for 'hedge' and 'fisrt' for 'first'.

This difficulty must be distinguished from inattention, clumsiness, poor comprehension, or poor hearing, all of which can give rise to some of the same behaviour. A comprehensive assessment of a child's abilities, as described in Chapter 2, provides many opportunities to determine whether a child has significant difficulties with sequential organization and to exclude other causes of similar behaviour.

Helping your child with sequential organization

Children with difficulties in this area are often helped by having a fairly set routine. A regular course of events helps the child to anticipate the next activity and remember the schedule. Set routines are particularly helpful for children who have difficulty understanding a verbal or written schedule, but who can get to know a routine if they are actively involved in following it.

A wallchart, with the day's programme pictorially represented, is often helpful for children with a poor sense of time sequence. Your child may find the chart easiest to understand if there is a separate sheet of paper for each day of the week and only one day is put up at a time. Make the chart as attractive as possible, and use colours to show up differences as well as correspondences in the schedules.

Teaching your child the order of the letters of the alphabet can be done by you and your child saying the letters alternately. When he is able to do this well, you say two consecutive letters each, then three, and so on.

It is often helpful to teach lists by setting them to a tune. There is a well-known tune for the months of the year, but other lists, such as the days of the week and the order of the seasons, can all be set to music using well-known tunes. There are tapes available of the multiplication tables set to music for children.

Try to find ways of making it easier for your child to follow a set of instructions, such as by using colour coding, word and story associations, and mnemonics.

Find ways in which he can have practice with schedules, such as using the television guide, looking up numbers in the telephone directory, or keeping a diary.

You can also let him cook simple things he enjoys (such as fudge), by following a recipe step by step. He should also be encouraged to tell you stories about what has happened to him during the day, and to repeat jokes he has heard. All these activities enhance sequencing skills.

11
Coordination and clumsiness

Rachel is eight years old. She was slow to crawl and walk. She still cannot pedal a tricycle, fasten small buttons, or tie her laces. She is very poor at sports and is often teased by the other children for her awkward running style. She is a messy eater and washes herself and brushes her teeth with great difficulty. Her mother says that she has a poor sense of direction and still confuses right with left. Rachel's school work is satisfactory. Her writing is untidy, but if she prints slowly it is legible.

Rachel has been tested by a psychologist and found to have some visual perception difficulties, but to be of normal intelligence. Her reading, spelling, and arithmetic are in the average range. A paediatrician has examined Rachel and detected no abnormalities that can account for her clumsiness.

The term 'clumsiness' will be used in this chapter to refer to unexplained, significant difficulties in the coordination of movement in a child of average, or above average, intelligence.

This sort of clumsiness is commonly associated with other forms of specific learning difficulty, such as reading difficulty. This does not mean, however, that most children with specific learning difficulty are clumsy. Many are, in fact, well coordinated. But clumsiness is far more common in children with specific learning difficulty than in other children.

Clumsiness is more common in boys and quite often runs in families.

How coordination is assessed

The word 'motor' is used for movement. *Gross motor skills* involve large groups of muscles responsible for activities such as walking, running, jumping, hopping, and bicycle riding. *Fine motor skills* involve the hands and fingers, and are concerned with activities such as writing, drawing, using scissors, and tying knots.

There are a number of standardized tests of both gross and fine motor proficiency. These may be performed by a physiotherapist, an occupational therapist, or a doctor.

Activities must be carefully observed to detect the presence of tremors and other unusual movements. Balance, strength, tone, reflexes, and ability to interpret certain sensations are all assessed. It is essential that rare, serious conditions associated with poor coordination are excluded by a doctor. Children who are clumsy must also be differentiated from those who drop or damage objects because of difficulties with attention.

Types of clumsiness

There are four types of clumsiness, each associated with a different problem. These are movement planning impairment (dyspraxia), difficulty in localizing body position (agnosia), difficulty with direction (visual–spatial deficit), and low tone. I shall describe each one separately.

Movement planning deficit (dyspraxia)

In dyspraxia there is an impairment in the brain's control of purposeful movements. A child with dyspraxia can carry out individual movements, but has difficulty co-ordinating these movements in order to perform a particular task.

Dyspraxia is a common cause of clumsiness. Children with dyspraxia may also have speech difficulties (verbal dyspraxia) and occasionally have a tendency to dribble saliva because of poor swallowing control.

Agnosia

Agnosia refers to difficulties in processing information about bodily sensations. Children who have agnosia have difficulty judging the position of parts of their body in space. This may cause clumsiness.

One of the common tests for agnosia involves asking the child to tell the position of his fingers when they are moved by the examiner. The child keeps his eyes closed and is reliant on his brain interpreting information coming from the fingers.

As we carry out an action, our brain must continually process incoming sensations to judge the position of the moving parts of our body (head, neck, and limbs) at any moment in time. Our brain must do this quickly, and automatically initiate appropriate small muscular contractions and relaxations to fine-tune the action so that it can be carried out in a smooth and competent manner. In children with agnosia this does not occur, and movements are awkward and inaccurate.

Visual–spatial deficit

Whereas agnosia is a difficulty in sensing where the body is in space without using the eyes, visual–spatial deficit is a difficulty in direction sense when using the eyes. Agnosia may be thought of as a difficulty with 'inner space', visual–spatial deficit as difficulty with 'outer space'.

Visual–spatial deficit will result in difficulties in tasks such as telling right from left and following a map. It is also a cause of clumsiness in complex actions such as tying shoe laces, drawing pictures, and catching a ball.

There are special tests that assess visual–spatial skills. These usually involve tasks such as copying and arranging shapes.

Low tone

Although low tone is often given as a reason for a child's clumsiness, it is probably not a common cause of clumsiness.

Tone (or muscular tone, as it is properly called) refers to the resistance that muscles give to being moved when they are relaxed. This is ascertained by the examiner when he or she moves the child's limbs while the child keeps them as relaxed as possible. It should be distinguished from muscular weakness, which involves active contraction of the muscle by the child. Low tone, or 'hypotonia', signifies that the muscles give less resistance to passive movement, that is, they are floppier than normal.

The tone of the muscles is controlled by tiny 'stretch receptors' situated in their tendons. These in turn are controlled by the brain. Hypotonia is a common finding in children with clumsiness, but the cause is unknown.

Severe hypotonia can cause clumsiness, as it is difficult to control very floppy muscles, but mild hypotonia does not seem to be a problem. Many well-coordinated children have mild hypotonia, so it is difficult to accept that mild hypotonia on its own is a cause of clumsiness.

Many of the exercises to 'strengthen tone' are of questionable value. Exercises may increase the strength of the muscles, but probably have little effect on their tone.

Flat feet caused by low tone are often given as a cause of clumsiness. In the past, too much significance was given to flat feet. Flexible flat feet do not cause problems (high arches are more troublesome). As many as 10 per cent of normal school-age children have flat feet and these, like other low-tone manifestations, get better with time. Supports, special shoes, and exercises are of questionable value.

Treatment of clumsiness

The involvement of an occupational therapist or physiotherapist in providing advice about teaching children motor tasks is helpful. An occupational therapist will usually provide help with fine motor difficulties, and a physiotherapist with improving gross motor skills.

The first step is to identify tasks that are important to the child, such as catching a ball. The child will be motivated if he is learning a skill that is important to him. A realistic goal must be set at the outset.

The task should then be broken up into steps. Each step is usually taught separately, with praise for effort. It is best if the training is approached in an enjoyable manner, with tasks turned into games whenever possible. Each step is first introduced in an easy way and then gradually becomes more difficult (for example, when teaching catching, the child first catches a balloon, then a large ball, then smaller and smaller balls). Sometimes parallel exercises are useful, for example, the child practises clapping hands as a way of bringing the hands accurately together in preparation for catching a ball.

When teaching complex actions, such as tying shoe laces, it may be best to teach the last stage first. The parent ties the laces except for the last step, and then teaches the child to do this. When this is mastered the child learns to do the last two steps, and so on, until the child can do the whole process himself. This form of teaching is known as 'reverse chaining'.

In all motor tasks it is essential that the child practises repeatedly. It is also important that the actions taught are directly related to the desired skill; it is no use practising kicking a bag to become better at catching it.

It is very important that the child is allowed to practise these motor tasks in private, away from his peers (and sometimes away from his siblings too). It is only when he has mastered the skill that he should have the opportunity of displaying his ability in public. It is best if you can arrange this in a way that your child will be rewarded for his accomplishment.

Helping your child with visual–spatial difficulties

If your child has difficulties telling his right from his left, help him by playing games such as 'Simon says' ('Simon says touch your head with your right hand, and so on') and 'Looby Lou' ('Put your left foot in, take your right foot out, and so on'). Mazes and treasure hunts with instructions such as 'take five steps to the left' are helpful. If your child makes a coloured mark on his right hand each day, this may help him to remember which hand is which. Thinking of his left arm as his 'watch arm' may be useful if he wears a watch.

If your child finds tying his own shoe laces, or knotting his tie, extremely difficult, then teaching these skills may have to be postponed for a while. In the meantime, Velcro fastenings on shoes, and 'pre-knotted' ties that clip on to his collar, can be a great help.

Give him practice with doing puzzles and mazes, as well as copying drawings. The books of children's puzzles with tasks such as mazes, 'join the dots', and 'spot the hidden figures' are excellent ways of developing these skills.

12
Social and emotional development

There is widespread recognition that children with specific learning difficulties may experience social and emotional problems *because* of their learning difficulties, but it is often not realized that impairment of social skills may itself be a form of learning difficulty. This is due to a limitation in the way that the brain is able to understand social conventions. This is called a social cognition (or social learning) deficit.

In this chapter, I shall first discuss social cognition deficit, and then discuss a number of behaviour problems that may occur as a result of a specific learning difficulty.

Social cognition deficit

Social skills, like any other skills, have to be learned. Yet much of what children learn about socially appropriate behaviour is not actually taught to them; they simply pick it up as they go along.

Some children of normal intelligence seem to be less able to learn these things, even when taught. This may be their only area of difficulty, but it is commonly associated with other learning difficulties.

These children have been accurately described as being 'socially tone deaf'. They do not pick up the same cues as other children of the same age. They do not seem to predict the social consequences of their actions. They may be uninhibited, undressing in public without the same embarrassment that their peers would experience. They may be overfriendly to strangers. They may frequently say very tactless things without realizing the effect they are having. They often do not read facial expressions and are oblivious to whether someone is angry or upset with them. They may kiss classmates at an age where this is no longer appropriate. They may make unusual sounds in public. They may be insatiable in their activities, not knowing when to stop in the way another child of their age would.

Although such behaviour may be apparent to all who meet the child, the people who are most likely to notice it are the child's peers. With them, the child often sticks out like a sore thumb. This is something that may not be apparent if the child is only observed in a one-to-one relationship at a clinic.

It is typical of such children that they have little or no insight into how differently they are perceived. They do not seem to be able to learn the skills that are required to mix with others. They often become loners, or play with children younger or older than themselves. With younger children, they blend in because of their immaturity. With older children, more allowances are often made for their inappropriate behaviour.

These problems are usually very distressing for parents. This may be compounded by not realizing that the child's behaviour is not the parents' fault. These children need to be taught social skills but, as is the case with any form of specific learning difficulty, progress is often slow.

Many health centres and adolescent units now run social skills training groups where children can learn to become better at understanding the social consequences of their actions. They can also acquire techniques for interpreting social cues and for being accepted by peers.

Parents can play a role by tactfully pointing out ways in which the child could win friends. It may be helpful to rehearse certain situations with your child so that he learns how to act in those situations. This can be done so that it is an enjoyable experience.

You may need to take an active role in arranging for another child to play with your child after school. If your child is too shy to invite a prospective friend home to play, arrange this with the child's parents. Once your child's confidence increases, your involvement will no longer be necessary. Children usually get on better in groups of two, rather than three.

Such children usually need work at improving their self-esteem and coping with teasing. If a child is being teased, particularly in certain situations such as the bus stop or the swimming pool, there may be some action that can be taken to avoid this. The help of the teacher can be very productive in these situations.

Behaviour that may arise because of a specific learning difficulty

Many children with a specific learning difficulty adjust well to their disability. Others may have one of a number of emotional difficulties. Whether a child experiences emotional or social difficulties depends on not only his temperament but also the nature of his disability.

Children who have difficulties in academic areas and are also clumsy are more likely to suffer than children who have difficulty in only one sphere of their lives. The environment in which the child finds himself also has an important part to play in determining how he will cope with his difficulties. Although parents play an important role in this regard, children experience many stresses that lie beyond their parents' control. Other children, teachers, relatives, and society in general, play an important part in determining how a child sees himself and how he copes. In addition, the help available to a child, both in school and out, often varies greatly from one place to another.

There follow some common behaviours seen in children with specific learning difficulties as they attempt to cope with their disability. The advice on managing these behaviours is intended as a general guide, and should be read in conjunction with the advice in the section on building up your child's self-esteem (Chapter 4).

School avoidance

Some children with specific learning difficulty enjoy school. Many do not, but nevertheless go reluctantly. A small proportion dislike school so much that they avoid going. This may take a number of forms. The child may flatly refuse to leave home, he may frequently complain that he is ill, he may pretend he is going off to school but never arrive, or he may leave school during the course of the day by absconding or by saying he is ill.

Those who complain of being ill may be feigning illness, or they may be so anxious about going to school that they actually experience stress-related symptoms such as abdominal pain and headache.

This sort of school avoidance is usually due to distress over the academic or social difficulties experienced by the child. He may be frightened of failing, or of being teased or ostracized. Sometimes the child tries to avoid particular lessons: for example, mathematics in the case of a child with arithmetic difficulty, or physical education in a clumsy child. Parents may see a pattern in the days the child misses.

A distinction should be drawn between this sort of school avoidance and the intense fear of school (school phobia) that is often associated with issues related to leaving home, rather than anxiety about school itself.

If your child is avoiding school, speak to him about it. You should also speak to his teacher to see if there are academic or social stresses that can be ameliorated.

It is important to prevent school avoidance becoming a regular pattern of behaviour. If you feel your child is feigning illness, do not give him excessive attention. Give him bland food when he is at home and do not let him spend all the time watching the TV. Be matter-of-fact and encourage attendance at school, even if only for half the day. It is important to keep in touch with the school and have work sent home that he is expected to do. There should be a clear expectation that he returns to school at the earliest possible opportunity, which will happen in most cases.

If these simple measures do not work, it is best to involve your child's doctor or a psychologist. This is particularly important if your child is refusing to leave his room or is very withdrawn.

Homework avoidance

Many children with specific learning difficulty do not do their homework. This is often a cause of family tension. If your child is not completing his homework, you should first check whether it is too difficult, or too much, for him. If so, speak to his teacher about this.

If the level and amount of homework is appropriate, but your child is still having difficulties, you may need to look at how he goes about doing the work. Do not be tempted to do the work for him, but help him to learn how to organize himself in an efficient manner. You will need to look at when he does the homework, where he does it, and how he arranges the time to do it.

It is usually best if there is a specified homework time. For some children (such as those with attention difficulties) this might need to follow a chance to burn off energy in active play. For other children, it may be better to leave the play as a reward for after the homework is completed. Whichever time is chosen, there should be some specified reward for when the work is completed. The child needs as quiet an environment as possible. Many children work best if there is a parent nearby, even though he or she may not need to take an active part in helping the child. For such children, the parent's presence has a settling effect on the child. Homework should not go on for too long. If there is a lot of work to cover, or your child is slow, it may need to be broken up into a couple of sessions.

It is important that you teach your child how to manage his time effectively. He needs to know how to arrange work according to priorities, and how to work systematically. Teach him not to expect you to do the work for him, but to think of you as a resource that he can call upon when he needs advice.

Children may need particular help if a project has to be completed over a long period of time. Help your child to break this into stages and to create a timetable that shows when each stage will be completed. Without this help, things will often be left to the last minute and the child then feels overwhelmed.

TV 'addiction'

Parents of children with specific learning difficulty often complain that their child spends a lot of his time when he gets home watching TV. Difficulties with academic work, as well as with social relationships, mean that TV is a common diversion for this group of children.

Limiting the amount of time the child spends watching TV is only part of the answer. It is important to try to find rewarding activities to replace watching the TV. You may be able to find after-school activities for your child, based on his interests. The local child health centre may be able to suggest appropriate activities in your area. Keep an eye on local newspapers and talk to other parents to find out about suitable activities for children. There are guides to activities for children published in some places. You may also obtain information from local sports and recreation centres. If your child is having difficulty making friends, he may benefit from attending a social skills group. You will need to check with your local health centre whether one is being run in your area.

Cheating

Another behaviour that children may learn in order to cope with failure is cheating. This may occur at school, when work is copied, or at home. First, you should make certain that your child is not being set tasks that are beyond his capabilities. You should also make certain that he is not receiving criticism for his failure. A child should be praised for his effort, even if his work is incorrect.

If teachers spot that a child is cheating they should only mark the portions of the work that they feel the child has done himself and ignore the rest. In this way he learns that he is rewarded only for his own efforts.

It is best if you do not let your child get away with lying or cheating. Whenever he is caught at it, ask him if he understands what he is doing. Explain that you admire his efforts whether he succeeds or fails, but that cheating spoils games and work. Talk to him about this, mentioning that you understand why he wants to cheat, but explaining how much better it is to be honest. Ensure that honesty is praised. In games set him an example of how to lose gracefully.

Aggression

Aggressive behaviour is often a cover for low self-esteem. A child who feels he has failed may vent his anger on others. A child who does not feel good about himself may derive satisfaction from exerting power over others. Such a child may get into fights, bully other children, or engage in arguments and make critical remarks about his siblings and others.

Listen carefully to what your child says when he insults others; he is probably echoing the criticisms that hurt him the most. If this is the case, you may need to check on why he feels that he is being criticized in this way and take steps to stop it. Check whether he is being victimized at school. He may be part of a pecking order and simply acting out the aggression he is experiencing.

Determine whether he is behaving in an aggressive manner only in certain situations and see if you can identify what provokes the behaviour. Often, outbursts occur at times when your child feels failure, or the threat of failure. It may be possible to avoid such situations, or to change things so that your child does not feel inadequate.

For some children, it may be necessary to arrange a reward system for not losing their temper. You should also teach your child strategies for coping with his aggressive feelings. He may go for a walk, jump on a trampoline, or listen to music. Sometimes a child will benefit from a punchbag, or even a pillow, on which he can vent his anger. Encourage him to express to you the way he feels and accept these feelings with sympathy.

If aggressive outbursts remain a problem, despite these measures, it is a good idea to seek help from your child's doctor or psychologist. If a habit of resorting to aggressive outbursts becomes engrained it may be difficult to eradicate later and may cause much trouble in adulthood.

Controlling behaviour

This is seen when children cope with their difficulties by trying to dominate others. They tell people what to do, defy adults, and generally seek to dominate and control situations.

The best way to manage such behaviour is to give the child some areas where he does have control, for example choosing his clothes, helping to select items at the supermarket, and deciding how to spend his pocket money (within reason!). Allocate some pleasant task that becomes his responsibility and reward him for doing it. Explain to him that certain tasks are his domain, but others are not.

When giving him instructions, do this in the form of choices whenever possible: 'Do you want to tidy up your room while I do the lounge, or will you do the lounge while I do your room?'. This is less likely to make him feel that he is losing autonomy.

Quitting

Some children develop a habit of quitting as a way of coping with their difficulty. In school work and in games, they give up the moment they encounter difficulties and often refuse to continue.

If your child behaves in this manner you should first talk to him about the importance of persevering. Tell him stories about great people who did not give up when they were facing defeat. Children's libraries often have books with stories that teach children particular virtues like courage or persistence.

Make certain that the tasks that your child has to accomplish are within his capabilities, and give him rewards for accomplishment. You could give him some special job to do that requires persistence and have a reward system for when he finishes it. In this way he will have the opportunity to learn that persistence does pay.

Withdrawal

Some children with a specific learning difficulty respond to their disability by retreating. They may avoid contact with those outside the family. This behaviour may be a manifestation of lack of social skills or depression.

It is usually best to obtain professional advice from a doctor or psychologist. Children who lack social skills may benefit from attending a social skills training group. They may also benefit from talking about their difficulties to a counsellor. Sometimes the child can be introduced gradually to activities that he will enjoy, but this should be planned carefully. Collaborating with another child on a project may be a way of building up confidence in socialization.

Occasionally, the difficulties experienced by a child lead to depression. Parents may fail to recognize the signs of depression because of their reluctance to come to terms with the fact that their child is depressed.

Symptoms of depression include feelings of sadness, loneliness, and isolation, self-deprecatory remarks, sleep disturbance, and complaints of boredom. Any of these symptoms may occur transiently in a child who is not suffering from depression but, if prolonged or intense, professional help should be sought. Talk of suicide should *always* be taken seriously.

Sometimes, depression is difficult to recognize because it is 'masked', that is, hidden behind some protective behaviour. Masked depression may manifest itself with bodily symptoms (such as headaches), eating disturbance, aggressive and rebellious behaviour, deterioration in school performance, and drug or alcohol abuse.

A child who seems depressed should be seen by a doctor and may need to be referred for psychiatric help.

Part 3

Controversial treatments

First and foremost, do no harm.
Hippocrates (460–377 BC)

There are no quick and easy ways of overcoming a specific learning difficulty, but conventional management, as outlined in this book, will always bring results eventually.

When there is no effective cure for a condition, numerous dubious 'cures' arise. The existence of a number of so-called cures is usually a sign that no single one is effective. An effective treatment quickly displaces all others.

Some of these treatments are a waste of time and money that could be spent more profitably in other ways to benefit the child. Some may be harmful to the physical and psychological well-being of the child. Some may have detrimental effects on the family as a whole.

It is important, therefore, that you obtain reliable information from your doctor or psychologist before becoming involved in any treatment. Do not rely on stories of miraculous cures from those who promote these treatments. Evaluations should be by controlled trials published in reputable journals. Such trials should be carried out 'blind' whenever possible, meaning that the person who assessed the performance of children both on and off the treatment did not know which had received treatment and which had not until after the assessments were completed. If the treatment consists of a medicine, the untreated group should have received a dummy medicine (placebo) to make the comparison valid. In addition, the person who carried out the trial should not have had any vested interest in the treatment.

An increasing number of independent trials of controversial treatments are now reported in scientific journals. In addition, professional and government bodies often make policy statements about certain treatments based on reviews of scientific data.

If you plan to start a treatment, first be certain that you understand the risks involved. Decide upon what objective improvement you wish to see, and how long it should take before this occurs. If the objective improvement is not achieved, treatment should cease. Do not allow yourself to accept some vague qualitative improvements decided upon at a later date. Children with specific learning difficulties always develop new skills, and usually do so in sudden spurts followed by periods of consolidation. Such changes should not be ascribed to a particular treatment unless they are exceptional.

Sensory integrative therapy

This form of therapy is based on the work of A. Jean Ayers, an occupational therapist, who believed that learning problems were related to difficulties in processing incoming stimuli. She also believed that the development of higher intellectual processes is dependent on primitive parts of the brain developing first.

The therapy consists of manoeuvres such as getting the child to spin, ride a scooter down a ramp, swing, and crawl. It also involves stimulating the child's skin with materials of various textures and a battery-operated brush.

It is questionable whether such techniques influence a child's learning in academic areas. Ayers claimed that children treated by her methods made exceptional academic gains, but this has not been confirmed by independent workers.

On the basis of both theoretical considerations, and the evidence, it seems highly unlikely that a child can learn a complex skill, such as reading, by riding a scooter or swinging. Time spent on such manoeuvres is probably better utilized giving the child practice at the specific skill that he needs to learn, whether that is spelling or buttoning his shirt. Sensory integration programmes that involve activities such as spinning and creeping may be humiliating for some children.

Doman–Delacato method (patterning)

This method, like sensory integrative therapy, is based on beliefs about the importance of primitive parts of the brain and perceptual training in learning. It was devised at the Institute for the Achievement of Human Potential by Glenn Doman, a physiotherapist, and Carl Delacato, an educator.

The method of treatment is very intensive. An individualized programme is prepared for each child, which may occupy most of the child's time at home. A variety of manoeuvres are carried out on the assumption that by manipulating the head and limbs to stimulate certain primitive movements (patterning), the brain will undergo 'neuronal (nerve cell) organization'. Both the theory of neuronal organization and the claims for the treatment are open to question.

The programme is very intensive, and for some children the parents have to gather a circle of helpers. Treatment includes activities such as swinging the child, getting him to crawl, hanging him upside-down, flashing lights in his eyes, stimulating his skin with materials of various textures, subjecting the child to certain noises, getting the child to rebreathe expired air in a mask, and restricting the intake of fluid and certain foods. There is also emphasis on dominance training (see later in this chapter).

Some of the vigorous and continuous movements to which the child's body is subjected may be exhausting and painful for him, and there is concern in some quarters that this treatment may cause him excessive suffering. A number of professional bodies have expressed serious reservations about this form of therapy.

Allergy

There is no doubt that allergy-induced illness, such as asthma and hayfever, may cause a child's school work to suffer because of absenteeism, or the child feeling below par. Whether learning difficulty can itself be a form of allergic reaction, as is suggested in some quarters, is unlikely. Those who make such claims have not produced satisfactory evidence to support their assertion.

The practice of putting children with specific learning difficulties on allergy diets to improve their performance or behaviour is controversial. The reliability of blood and skin tests for allergy in these children is also questionable.

If a child is put on an allergy diet, this should be supervised by a doctor to ensure that the child is receiving adequate nutrition. The best way to evaluate the diet is for an independent observer, such as the teacher, to monitor the child's performance without knowing when he is on the allergy diet and when he is eating normally. It is important that the observation extends over a period when the child is on a normal diet, then on the allergy diet, and is finally back on a normal diet again. The child's learning should improve on the allergy diet and deteriorate when the normal diet is recommenced.

If a child is on a diet, he should still receive conventional educational help according to his needs.

Children with specific learning difficulties are sometimes put on a gluten-free diet in an attempt to help solve their problem. Gluten is a protein found in wheat, rye, and oats. The only condition known to be associated with gluten sensitivity is coeliac disease, a condition unrelated to specific learning difficulties. Coeliac disease should only be diagnosed by a paediatric gastroenterologist (a specialist in the stomach and intestines of children).

Visual training

'Developmental' optometrists believe that many forms of specific learning difficulty, particularly specific reading difficulty, are primarily due to visual impairment. For this reason they may undertake long and complex eye examinations and prescribe eye exercises (visual training) to improve the way the eyes work.

Organizations such as the American Academy of Pediatrics have stated that there is no evidence that such treatments have any beneficial effect on a child with a specific learning difficulty, and that they may cause unnecessary expense and delay appropriate help for the child.

A child with a specific learning difficulty should have a conventional eye examination by an ophthalmologist (an eye specialist) to exclude conditions such as longsightedness or short-sightedness that may aggravate the child's difficulties. Such visual problems may make it difficult for a child to see letters clearly; however, eye defects are not responsible for difficulties such as reversal of letters, words, or numbers. These errors do not originate in the eyes, but in the brain.

Tinted lenses

Helen Irlen, an educational psychologist from California, was the first to claim that tinted glasses could help children with specific reading difficulty. She described a 'scotopic sensitivity syndrome', characterized by headaches, itchy eyes, and difficulty in reading. To treat this, the child is tested with transparencies of different colours to find the 'correct' tint. The claims for this form of treatment have not been confirmed by controlled trials.

Hypoglycaemia diets

'Hypoglycaemia' means low blood sugar. There are those who believe that this is a common cause of all kinds of learning and behaviour difficulties. They usually treat this with diets high in protein and complex carbohydrates.

True hypoglycaemia is a very rare condition and is not associated with specific learning difficulties. There is no evidence that antihypoglycaemia diets improve specific learning difficulties.

Laterality training

As mentioned in Chapter 1, Dr Samuel T. Orton first proposed failure of dominance as the cause of specific learning difficulties. This theory was critically discussed in Chapter 3.

Since Dr Orton's time, there have been many who have tested for evidence of laterality and utilized this in therapy. Such treatment forms part of some of the other perceptual training programmes, such as sensory integrative therapy and the Doman–Delacato method. It is also practised by many educators and therapists who adopt a more conventional approach.

Laterality training may take many forms, such as patching the 'non-dominant' eye, active training of the 'dominant' hand, and even discouraging a child from hearing non-verbal music in the belief that this will stimulate the 'non-dominant' side of the brain.

In Chapter 3, I commented on how unreliable tests of laterality are, and how dominance and laterality have a far more complex relationship than is often realized. There is certainly no evidence that laterality training is beneficial to children with specific learning difficulties. Time spent in the testing of laterality, and training of 'dominance', would be better spent on more conventional methods of teaching desired skills.

Megavitamins and mineral therapy

High doses of vitamins and minerals are another treatment suggested for children with specific learning difficulties. This sort of treatment is advocated by those calling themselves orthomolecular physicians (or orthomolecular psychiatrists).

Although there are some rare inborn disorders that respond to certain vitamins, specific learning difficulties are not among them. Trials of high doses of vitamins have not been shown to improve learning. In fact, some vitamins can accumulate in the body and have toxic effects, slowing down the child's development, and causing ill-health and even death.

Orthomolecular physicians often analyse hair to obtain a 'profile' of vitamin and mineral 'deficiencies'. The levels regarded as abnormal by many of these physicians would usually be considered quite acceptable by other doctors.

Chiropractic

Chiropractors use manipulation of the spine as a method of treating disease. This form of treatment has not been shown to help children with specific learning difficulties.

Adulthood

*I was happy as a child with my toys in the nursery. I have been
happier every year since I became a man. But this interlude of
school makes a sombre, grey patch upon the chart of my journey.*
My Early Life, Sir Winston Churchill

All children with specific learning difficulties improve as
they grow. In some, the difficulties resolve completely, while
others continue to have some degree of difficulty in the
specific areas of learning affected. We still have no way of
determining which children will continue to experience
difficulty and which will not. Nor do we have reliable
figures on the relative proportions of those where the
difficulties resolve completely and those where they persist.

This chapter provides information and advice for
adults with persisting specific learning difficulties.

The advantage of adulthood

Many people are designed to be better adults than children. A child has little opportunity of selecting those
things that he enjoys or finds easier, and to avoid those he
dislikes or finds difficult. He is required to be an all-
rounder, performing a wide range of activities, many
under the critical scrutiny of his teachers and peers. It is
daunting to think of what many children are required to
do regularly at school: reading aloud, writing something
that will be marked (for content, neatness, and spelling),

doing arithmetical computations that will be checked, playing competitive sport, performing in a play in public, and playing a musical piece to a critical audience. An adult, on the other hand, can have a successful career and avoid any, or all, of these activities.

Many famous people are said to have had a specific learning difficulty as children, but it is very difficult to know for certain if this is true. Nevertheless, many of their stories are highly suggestive of the condition. What they all show, whether they had a specific learning difficulty or not, is that problems with learning in childhood need not be a bar to outstanding achievements in adulthood. There follow some examples.

Hans Christian Andersen (1805–1875). Famous as an author of children's stories such as 'The Little Match-girl' and 'The Little Mermaid', his handwriting shows characteristics of specific learning difficulty.

Auguste Rodin (1840–1917). Now famous for his sculptures, such as 'The Thinker' and 'The Burghers of Calais', he was regarded as 'an idiot', and 'ineducable' as a child. Throughout his life, Rodin found academic skills such as spelling and arithmetic impossible to master.

Thomas Alva Edison (1847–1931). The inventor of the electric light bulb and the phonograph, and the holder of over 1300 other patents, he was thought to be a 'dunce' as a school boy. His teacher said he was 'addled' (confused) and he came bottom of the class. He never mastered basic skills in writing, spelling, and arithmetic. At 19, he wrote the following letter to his mother:

Dear mother
started store several weeks i have growed considerably I don't look much like a Boy now Hows all the fold did you receive a Box of Books Memphis that he promised to send them languages Your son Al

Harvey Cushing (1869–1939). A world famous medical researcher, brain surgeon, and author. Cushing won a Pulitzer prize in 1926 for his biography of Sir William Osler, despite being unable to spell the most elementary words. His manuscripts abound with spellings such as: 'definate', 'cronicling', and 'pharcical'.

Sir Winston Churchill (1874–1965). Britain's great politician, orator, historian, and winner of the Nobel Prize for Literature. His school reports show a boy failing miserably. His father despaired of him ('I have an idiot for a son'), and put him in the army class at Harrow. He failed there twice, but was given special coaching and then managed to gain a place at the Royal Military College at Sandhurst.

Albert Einstein (1879–1955). The greatest scientist of the twentieth century, he was capable of the most advanced thought but failed hopelessly at school, where he had great difficulty learning to read. (He was nine before he began to read.) Even as an adult, writing continued to be a great problem for him.

Paul Elvström (1929–). A world champion racing yachtsman, professional sailmaker, and expert yacht-racing tactician. Elvström, a coauthor of a number of books, has said of himself, 'I am word-blind. I can't read and I can't write. I get a headache and then I can't think. In school I was the worst in the class. I was not lazy, but I just couldn't read. It was such a big handicap for me'. Despite this disability, he won the World Championship in eight different classes, and earned four Olympic gold medals. His story, like that of Edison, is one of determination, not just talent. He won a World Championship with a broken leg still strapped up, and he would often jump into the cold sea before a race, fully clothed, to increase his weight and so give his boat extra ballast.

All these famous people demonstrate that, despite their special talents, they had great and unexplained difficulties with learning certain skills. In all, the school years were a time of great hardship because of the emphasis on these skills at this stage of life. Later they could overcome these difficulties, many becoming famous writers despite poor skills in handwriting and spelling. They all lived at a time when they could not benefit from an enlightened approach to their problem. Today, children experiencing such difficulties at school can be referred for an assessment to determine the nature of their difficulties and to plan ways of helping them.

Coming to terms with persisting specific learning difficulty

The first step for an adult with persisting difficulties in learning is to try to *accept* that he has such difficulties. This allows him to take appropriate steps to overcome them. As the short biographies above show, people who have difficulties with learning are in good company. They are by no means a small group, either. It is estimated that as many as two to three million adults in the UK, and 23 million in the USA, have significant difficulty with reading and writing. Not all of these have a specific learning difficulty, but many do.

An adult with a specific learning difficulty should tell people close to him about his condition. This avoids embarrassing situations and allows these people to provide appropriate support. On the other hand, it is not necessary to volunteer information about specific learning difficulty to a prospective employer, unless the difficulty means that the applicant will not be able to perform the job. To colleagues at work, it may be best just to say 'I am not a good reader', or 'I am not a good speller', although this is a matter for individual judgement.

Adults with a specific learning difficulty can continue to improve their basic skills throughout their life. It has been demonstrated again and again that it is never too late to learn. There are now a greater number of literacy courses for adults, or one can arrange to be taught in the privacy of one's own home.

If an adult with a specific learning difficulty is taking further training, he should tell lecturers, or teachers, about his condition. This will enable allowances to be made for his difficulties.

Getting around difficulties

There are many ways in which an adult with a specific learning difficulty can overcome his disabilities.

One of the important ways is to make use of aids that are available. At lectures, a tape recorder can be used if difficulty is experienced in taking notes, or a friend may be prepared to use carbon paper to make you a copy of his notes. An electric typewriter or computer can be a great help in producing work that is legible and well presented. A computer program may also be used to check spelling. For those who are better at typing than writing, portable computers and digital diaries can be carried around everywhere for recording information. Calculators are easily portable and have made arithmetical calculation easy for everyone. Spelling dictionaries, both electronic and in the form of books, are useful for adults with spelling difficulties. These were described in Chapter 6.

For those who have to take examinations, it is usually possible to arrange for allowances to be made for difficulties with reading or writing. It may be necessary to have a letter from a doctor or psychologist to obtain permission to use aids such as a typewriter, thesaurus, tape recorder, amanuensis, or spelling dictionary.

Those who continue to have difficulties with reading may benefit, from 'talking books' (recording of book readings) which are available from many libraries. Some libraries have books written for adults that are easy to read. Although reading is a great source of pleasure for many people, there are other ways to enjoy oneself in a constructive way. Many adults are kept sufficiently well informed by TV, radio, and movies.

Adults who have difficulty with reading or writing should not feel hesitant about asking someone to fill in forms for them. Many adults with good literacy skills have difficulties with forms. Similarly, when taking messages, there is no reason to be embarrassed about asking to have things repeated or spelt out.

Many poor readers and spellers develop their own word book, which they carry with them. They write down all the words they have difficulty with as they meet them. They then have them for reference or to commit to memory later.

Careers

There are no hard and fast rules about which careers are appropriate, or inappropriate, for people with specific learning difficulties. With determination, people can often bypass their difficulties. The widespread use of multiple-choice examinations means that assessment for knowledge, rather than literary ability, is now far more common.

A study in 1968 of children with specific learning difficulties found that 14 per cent became research scientists, 13 per cent business executives, 11 per cent university lecturers, 7 per cent school teachers, 7 per cent lawyers, and 7 per cent owners or managers of a business. Most of the children in this particular study came from families where one of the parents was a professional.

The best way to ensure that an appropriate career is chosen is with the aid of a careers adviser. Careers advisers may be available at school or at a vocational guidance centre. Some psychologists in private practice do aptitude testing and give vocational advice. Children should have such testing towards the end of high school.

In the UK, adults with specific learning difficulties may be able to apply to be registered as a disabled person. Under the 1944 Disabled Persons (Employment) Act, anyone who employs more than 20 people has to employ a specific number of people (3 per cent of the staff) who are registered as disabled. There are other regulations for employers with more than 250 employees in the Companies Act (1980). The Manpower Services Commission has produced a 'Code of Good Practice on the Employment of Disabled People' which may be obtained from Her Majesty's Stationery Office. Although many people with specific learning difficulties may not want to be registered as a disabled person, it could be a great help if difficulty is experienced in gaining employment.

In the USA, schemes vary from state to state. It is best to contact the regional office of your nearest Department of Education (ask for Rehabilitation Services).

In Australia, the Department of Industrial Relations has Vocational Services branches, and the Commonwealth Employment Service (CES) provides advice and special services for people with disabilities.

Conclusion

It is now over a hundred years since Dr Pringle Morgan reported the story of Percy; this was the first description of a child with a specific learning difficulty. Gradually, the concept of specific learning difficulties has evolved to account for the unexplained struggle of intelligent children, like Percy, to learn.

The pattern of difficulties seen in these children is now well recognized. Parents can, therefore, be reassured that their child does not have a serious disease, that the problems are real and not imaginary, that they are due to constitutional factors in the child, and that it is not their fault, nor the fault of their child.

Assessment of the nature of the child's difficulties is now far more precise. This makes possible more appropriate help and teaching. The greater awareness of the needs of such children has resulted in better provision of specialized teaching and a wider range of support.

The future will, no doubt, bring a greater understanding of why some children learn with ease, while others struggle to learn. The group of disorders we call specific learning difficulties will be separated gradually into a number of conditions, each with its own cause. This will lead to the development of more effective treatments.

For the present, there are no easy remedies for children with specific learning difficulties. But, as I have tried to show in this book, there is, nevertheless, a great deal that can be done to help them.

Appendix: Useful addresses

United Kingdom
British Dyslexia Association
98 London Road
Reading
Berkshire
RG1 5AU

Scottish Dyslexia Association
Unit 3
Stirling Business Centre
Well Green
Stirling
FK8 2DZ

Dyslexia Association of Northern
Ireland
28 Bedford Street
Belfast
County Antrim
BT2 2FE

United States of America
Association for Children with
Learning Disabilities
4156 Library Road
Pittsburgh
PA 15234

The Orton Dyslexia Society, Inc.
724 York Road
Baltimore
MD 21204

Australia
Association for Children with
Learning Disabilities
21–3 Belmore Street
Burwood 2134

Australian Federation of SPELD
Associations
c/o SPELD NSW
129 Greenwhich Road
Greenwich 2065

Canada
The Canadian Association for
Children and Adults with
Learning Disabilities
Maison Kildare House
323 Chapel Street
Ottowa
K1N 7Z2

New Zealand
New Zealand Federation of
Specific Learning Difficulties
Associations, Inc.
PO Box 28–119
Auckland

Republic of Ireland
Dyslexia Association of Southern
Ireland
19 Upper Mount Street
Dublin 2

South Africa
Southern African Association for
Children with Learning and
Educational Difficulties
Division of Specialized
Education
University of Witwatersrand
1 Jan Smuts Drive
Johannesburg 2050

Index